Certified

Also by Kim Antieau

Novels
The Blue Tail • Broken Moon • Butch
Church of the Old Mermaids • Coyote Cowgirl • Deathmark
The Desert Siren • The Fish Wife: an Old Mermaids Novel
The Gaia Websters • Her Frozen Wild • Jewelweed Station
The Jigsaw Woman • Mercy, Unbound
The Monster's Daughter • Ruby's Imagine
Swans in Winter • The Rift • Whackadoodle Times

Nonfiction
Answering the Creative Call • Counting on Wildflowers
The Old Mermaids Book of Days and Nights
The Old Mermaids Book of Days and Nights: A Year and a Day Journal • An Old Mermaid Journal
The Salmon Mysteries • Under the Tucson Moon

Short Story Collections
Entangled Realities (with Mario Milosevic)
The First Book of Old Mermaids Tales
Tales Fabulous and Fairy
Trudging to Eden

Chapbook
Blossoms

Cartoons
Fun With Vic and Jane

Blog
www.kimantieau.com

Certified
Learning to Repair Myself and the World in the Emerald City

Kim Antieau

Green Snake
PUBLISHING

Certified: Learning to Repair Myself and the World in the Emerald City by Kim Antieau

Copyright © 2014 by Kim Antieau

ISBN: 978-1-949644-27-2

All rights reserved.

No part of this book may be reproduced without written permission of the author.

Cover illustration © Tul Chalothonrangsee | Dreamstime.com

With special thanks to Nancy Milosevic.

http://www.kimantieau.com

Electronic editions of this book are available at your favorite ebook store.

Published by Green Snake Publishing
www.greensnakepublishing.com

for my fellow students

CONTENTS

Preface 9

How to Begin 11
First (Bad) Impressions 20
Science of Joy 35
In-Between 47
Inflexible Me, Part 1 53
Inflexible Me, Part 2 65
Jewelweed 75
Feeding the Dragon, Part 1 89
Feeding the Dragon, Part 2 101
Let Them Eat Cake 111
Getting Out 126
To Home 133
My Wound is Food 137
Audacious 149
Top of the World, Ma! 158
Healing 182

Appendix: *The Wild Keeper* 185
Bibliography 194

About the Author 196

Preface

In April of 2010, I sat in my living room in front of the television and watched in horror as oil spilled into the Gulf of Mexico from the Deepwater Horizon blowout. I felt helpless. I resolved then and there to do more to help bring myself and the world back from the brink of destruction. I had done environmental and social justice work since I was a kid, but I didn't feel as though I had achieved much of anything. I needed a new skill set. I decided to do what I usually did when I came to a crossroads in my life: go back to school.

I picked Antioch University in Seattle because it was only a four hour drive from where I lived, and it had a certificate program in ecological design. I needed 18 credits—six graduate classes—to get a certificate. For each class, I'd travel to Seattle once a month for three months for a full day. If I took two classes a semester, I'd be done in nine months.

For some loony reason, I thought going through this program would save my life, save the world, and help me get a job where I could do good work and earn a sustainable income. I am a writer, primarily a novelist, and I am a librarian. At the time I decided to go back to school, the publishing world was crashing and burning, and I was only working part-time as a librarian, selecting books from home.

What follows is my account of what happens when a 50-something woman goes back to school with the intent of saving the world and herself.

A year ago, I read this manuscript, and I quickly put it away. It felt too personal and too raw. Yet now I publish this in the hope that readers will relate to the story of someone who keeps trying, who keeps getting up—the story of someone who makes mistake after mistake and yet is learning to see her life as a success.

What happened during the year I went back to school was completely different from any of my expectations. I don't know why I still insist on having expectations since they are never met. Maybe this is a trait of a perennial control freak. I don't know. It was a year of magic and travail.

I don't talk much about the professors or other students in this book. I don't name them. I don't name my family members either. This book isn't about them. It's about my mistakes, my misconceptions, my revelations. My husband, Mario Milosevic, is named. He has given me permission to name names when it comes to him. He's always a great support to me.

Most of these chapters were culled from original pieces I posted at the time on my website. For the most part, I left them as they were originally published, but I did edit them for sense.

By the way, this is a story about me going to school to study permaculture and sustainable food systems, but it is not a book on permaculture or sustainable food systems. There are many great books on those topics. Check out some of the titles in my bibliography to get started.

Best wishes,
Kim Antieau

How To Begin

When the Deepwater Horizon drilling rig blew up in the Gulf of Mexico on Earth Day 2010, causing the worst environmental disaster in our country's history, I didn't know what to do. I was angry and depressed as I watched the disaster unfold. No one seemed to know what to do. I wondered, "Where are all the smart people who can fix stuff like this?"

Of course, "stuff like this" should have never happened in the first place. After decades of lax regulations and a kind of legal deification of big corporations, environmental and economic disasters *were* happening with increased frequency. We couldn't deny it.

What could I do? I called the President. I called my elected officials. I begged them to do something about the oil pouring into the Gulf. I asked them to stop relying on information from British Petroleum. I felt like I was watching one of those dystopian novels I had read as a teenager: like in *Brave New World* or *1984* where the corporations are the government and if they tell a lie long enough, it becomes the "truth."

I suddenly felt as though I had no useful skills. I was a writer and librarian. I had written a novel in response to Hurricane

Katrina *(Ruby's Imagine)*, but I couldn't see that it had changed anything in our world.

I worked part-time from home as a selector for our library. When the district remodeled the library where I was branch manager a few years back, I got sick from the chemical outgassing and hadn't been able to work full-time away from home since.

I had been a social and environmental activist most of my life, starting when I was in elementary school trying to save killdeer nests from marauding boys. But I couldn't point to any successes. Obviously my methods weren't working.

And I couldn't see how my skills as writer, librarian, or activist could help at this moment in history.

While oil gushed into the Gulf of Mexico, off the coast of the state where I was born, I felt the bell jar of depression and anxiety begin to fall.

One night I couldn't sleep. I had advocated for a sea change in this country for some time. As a culture, we seemed soullessly consumptive. I remembered recently being at a workshop where the facilitator figuratively shook her finger at us and told us we needed to change how we looked at the world; we needed to change our lives.

I grew quite irritated with her. How dare she tell me, a grown woman, how I should live my life? In that moment, I understood how other people probably felt when I began ranting about our consumer culture, the perils of capitalism, our dependence upon fossil fuels, or whatever other lecture I was giving to someone who had not asked for one.

I didn't want to lecture anymore. It wasn't effective. I didn't want to battle anymore either. It was absolutely ineffective. We couldn't sit around waiting for the government to tell us what to do. We couldn't wait for anyone to tell us what to do. No more waiting. No more talking.

But what could I actually do now?

CERTIFIED

I needed some practical skills.

I wanted to learn how people could live on this planet in our cities or out in the country and still be a part of the environment—not apart from it, not pariahs amongst the wild, but a part of the whole ecological community. Then I could help create places that were energy efficient and safe and healthy to human inhabitants and the surrounding environment.

I sat on the couch with my computer in front of me and began looking for places where I could learn these kinds of skills. I didn't want to get another master's degree; I already had two. I didn't want a Ph.D. I couldn't afford it, and I wasn't interested in teaching.

In the middle of the night, after hours of searching, I stumbled upon a nine-month certificate program in ecological planning and design in Seattle, Washington, two hundred plus miles north of where I lived. The program included electives in permaculture and food systems, another area of interest for me.

The next morning I talked it over with Mario. If I took the program over the next year, we could probably afford it if we got a loan, unless something drastic happened to our incomes. As I talked about it, I wondered if I was crazy.

When I was younger, I knew I was smart. I was sure that meant I could always take care of myself. When I got sick, all that assurance went out the window. Now I knew I could easily be one of those people who ended up homeless and living on the street. For some time, I had been looking for a way to get a more steady income—more steady than intermittent writing income—without changing my beliefs about living and working sustainably.

Maybe going back to school could do that for me. But I didn't want to drain my family—Mario and me—of any more of our finances.

What if going to school was just one more way to educate myself uselessly?

I made phone calls to the school and spoke with an advisor at admissions. We talked about the certificates. I told her my concerns about going to school and spending all this money and then not getting a job out of it. She didn't have a real answer to that. What could she say? "I guarantee you'll find work." That would have been nice, but it wouldn't have been honest.

Next I told her I only wanted to go to school if it was a green campus. She said it was. They didn't use pesticides, and they used green building practices: no-VOC paints and carpets (when carpeting was needed). She told me it was an old building, but they did the best they could.

I then wrote to the permaculture course instructor. I told him my life history in about a page: about my health, my grief over the state of the world, and my inability to figure out how to make a meaningful contribution. After I sent the email, I was embarrassed. How could I so easily tell a stranger about my life? I wasn't sure why I did it. I wanted these people to know life had not been easy for me. Illness and financial woes had taken a toll. But mostly I wanted them to know I hadn't succeeded at making anything better in the world, despite my best efforts.

I didn't tell him everything, of course. I didn't say that I struggled with anxiety and depression. Didn't tell him that sometimes incessant worry possessed me like some demented neurotic demon that I couldn't shake loose no matter what I did.

I didn't tell anyone these things, so why would I tell him?

I'd always had a touch of anxiety, even when I was a kid. When I was in my early twenties, I caught a glimpse of my diagnosis in the file on my shrink's desk: chronic depression. When I saw those two words, I felt as though I had been punched in the stomach. It sounded like a life sentence: chronic depression. Chronic meant it would never go away, right?

In my mid-twenties, a doctor told me I had something called environmental illness. She said I was essentially allergic to the world. This was devastating news. I loved the world. Now it was making me sick? I had to change everything about my life, she said. The way I ate, drank, dressed, lived.

I stopped drinking. I began eating organic foods. I tried to lessen my stress and take time to relax, but I was in college, working nearly full-time while going to school full-time. I didn't know how to relax.

The diagnosis evolved over the years. What I had was now called "multiple chemical sensitivities." (This is essentially what the workers and some residents in the Gulf now have. The doctors call it tilt: toxicant induced loss of tolerance.)

I didn't like any of the diagnoses I'd gotten over the years. They all felt like a curse, a life-sentence. As I tried to protect myself from "the world," my life felt more and more constrained. Less and less joyful.

And my incessant worrying got worse, coming and going until it seemed to settle in good and hard after my mother died two and a half years before I went back to school. Maybe that was because I started eating less healthy. Maybe it was because I had also lost two very close friends two years before that. Maybe it was because of the two surgeries I had had, although they had cleared my sinuses so that I could actually breathe through my nose for the first time in nearly fifteen years.

Maybe it was because I was now in my fifties and I felt like half of my life had been spent in illness. More than half.

I didn't know why I had this chronic anxiety. Doctors, acupuncturists, naturopaths, craniosacral therapists, all kinds of therapists, and shamans had not been able to help. It started to feel as though this unsustainable part of myself was hard-wired and there was no way to riven it from my real self—because I was sure my real true self did not cower in fear or anxiety because she couldn't get her mind right.

In any case, after the permaculture instructor read my email (where I didn't mention my anxiety), he asked me to call him. So I did.

We talked about his permaculture class and the program at his university. I told him I had worked on many environmental projects. I had also been part of the Sanctuary movement when I lived on the coast of Oregon—on the fringes of it while I was in a peace group there. I had organized and marched against the war in Iraq. I had sued my county after they illegally sprayed pesticides in front of my house. I had fought many battles, and I was tired. He talked about cultivating resilience. With my voice shaking with tears, I said, "I feel as though I have no more resilience."

"I promise you at the end of this," he said, "you will find your resilience again."

Maybe those weren't his exact words. But they were good words. I felt better. Like maybe this was for me.

As we talked, I felt as though I was speaking with someone who was like-minded. I realized I wanted to be around people who shared my world view again and who were willing to work for their communities. I didn't want to lead anyone anywhere or teach anyone anything. Not right now. I wanted to learn new skills. I wanted to learn to make a living doing something meaningful.

After our conversation concluded, I filled out an online application for the graduate certificate program. Part of the application included a five page essay about who I was and why I was drawn to this program.

I also filled out a financial aid form called FAFSA. I wasn't eligible for any grants—there weren't many for graduate students—but I might be eligible for a loan.

It was strange filling out the applications. To see once again where I'd been. Got my Bachelor of Science degree at Eastern Michigan University where my father had gotten his degree. Then my Master of Arts. I'd stayed at EMU because it was comfortable and because I got a gig as a graduate assistant teaching freshman English. I took a writing class at Michigan State University as my very last class for my Master of Arts degree. That was where I met writer Mario Milosevic. We married a year later at the Nichols Arboretum in Ann Arbor.

I'd worked at a kitchen cabinetry place during my college years. The building used to fill up with varnish fog. I'd run outside to get away from it. I thought it was toxic stuff, but my boss would get angry if I said anything about it. She said that was what they did, and if I didn't like it I needed to quit.

I should have quit. I've spent many nights since wondering if working there was what damaged me.

I kept working there for a year after Mario and I got married, until we moved to the coast of Oregon to make our way in the world as freelance writers. I worked at a restaurant and then ran a food co-op for a while. Both of those jobs ended badly. So I became library director at a tiny library. Two years later, we moved to Arizona where I went to library school.

I developed terrible allergies and asthma during the year we lived in Tucson. I hated living there. I remember seeing students walking across the campus lawns as a man in a HAZMAT suit rode atop an herbicide-spraying machine. I remember the Catalinas turning red every evening from air pollution. I couldn't wait for the year to end so we could get back to the Pacific Northwest.

Where everything got worse.

Now, I was worried that going back to school would worsen my health problems again.

But I couldn't focus on that. That was all in the past. Going to school was an affirmative step in the right direction. Or at least in a new direction. Maybe I would finally find a sustainable and healthy way to make a living. Maybe I would actually get well again. Or for the first time.

Soon enough I had an appointment with the director for June 1. She needed to interview me before I was admitted. Because the weather was so bad that day, I asked if we could change it to a phone interview. I didn't relish driving in a torrential rainstorm for four hours. In the twenty-three years that I had lived here, I had never cancelled an appointment because of the rain.

At the appointed time, the phone rang, and we began our interview. The director wanted to know why I had chosen her school. Then she talked about their view of teaching. Instructors didn't act as "sages on stages" but as "guides on the sides." Part of the purpose of the program was to teach people about effective collaboration. Group work was essential.

I told her I had had bad experiences working in groups. First there had been the food co-op in Bandon, Oregon. My bosses had been the co-op board: twelve of the most dysfunctional people I had ever met. They seemed to think because it was a food co-op and they believed in peace and love that everything would turn out well. When one of the board members went psycho and threatened me in front of the entire board, with spit spewing, cigarette in one hand and finger poking at me with the other hand, not one of them did a thing to stop him or protest his behavior.

I later had to call the police on this board member, and I resigned as manager of the co-op.

That was my most troublesome experience with group work. The director suggested we could learn as much from bad experiences with groups as we could from the more successful ones. She suggested I write down my group experiences before beginning the program to see what I had learned. I agreed that would be a helpful exercise.

I told her I was quite willing and eager to work in groups. I wanted to learn how to collaborate more effectively. I had become a bit of a lone wolf. I wrote alone. I did my library work alone. I had come to believe I worked better alone without all that pesky human interaction.

She also said that working online was very important to a student's learning experience. Since our classes only met once a month, we needed to keep in touch and collaborate via our online classrooms. I told her I was quite comfortable with computers.

At one point when we were talking, she said she didn't believe we would see any cultural changes in our lifetime. This work we did was for the long haul. We needed to realize this to keep our sanity. I didn't argue with her, but I thought, "I don't think we have time to wait for the long haul." I kept thinking of the oil gushing into the Gulf of Mexico.

When it was time for me to ask questions, I said, "I'm 54 years old, and I have white hair. Am I going to be out of place?"

She told me the average student was about 36 years old. I wouldn't be out of place, but I wouldn't be part of the majority.

I could live with that.

When I got off the phone, I realized I had been accepted to the program.

I grinned and called Mario.

I was ready to begin my adventures in the Emerald City.

First (Bad) Impressions

July 2010

I drove to Seattle for my first residency during a heat wave. It was a Friday. A roadside sign in Vancouver, Washington, flashed a smog alert. "Please reduce driving," it said. Damn. Here I was learning more about sustainability and permaculture, and I was driving during a smog alert.

I couldn't reasonably go back home. That would mean I'd have to quit my classes, so I kept driving. I sang out the Celtic *fath fith* to protect me, the car, and everyone else, and I headed north. (The fath fith a protection charm a Celtic shaman taught me.)

Like me, the AC in our car didn't do well on really hot days, and this day was no exception. It was a long four hour drive. Traffic was slow off and on. I was hot and sweaty and crossing my fingers the car didn't overheat.

I got to Seattle around 3:30 p.m. and headed into the university district. I was desperate to get inside someplace cool.

I parked the car in the sunny lot by a three-story house. I had made arrangements to stay in the Quaker apartment in Seattle. I got out of my hot car and stepped into stifling heat. City heat is different from country heat. At least in the country you can find a tree or a spot of ground to cool your soles. Or so I fantasized as I hurried to the entrance to my new abode. I looked for the key where the hostess told me it would be under a metal rabbit by the door.

It wasn't there.

I looked again even though I couldn't have missed it. I knocked on the door. No one answered.

What was I going to do now? I had food in the car that needed refrigeration. *I* needed refrigeration. Where could I go? I didn't know this city at all.

I had only been to Seattle a few times before this. I had never gotten a good sense of it. We didn't come to Seattle more often because the traffic was notoriously awful. It could take four hours to drive two hundred miles or it could take six, seven, or eight hours: depending upon traffic.

Now I couldn't sit out here in the sun waiting to see if the hostess ever came home.

I was just about to leave when another door opened and a woman leaned out of the house. I told her who I was and said the key wasn't where it was supposed to be.

"It's been a crazy day," she said. "I'll let you in."

A few moments later, the locked door opened, and I stepped into cool darkness. Ahhh. The woman led me down a very short hall.

"Someone just left," she said. "I haven't had time to change the sheets or clean."

"No hurry," I said.

The door was open so I could see inside the room as she made the bed and I waited in the hall. It looked more like a big closet than a bedroom. The woman handed me the keys. I went out to the car and began bringing in my things. A few minutes later, the hostess rushed out of the room, and I was able to squeeze in.

I wasn't certain what I had been expecting, but this wasn't it. I was thinking more apartment or hotel room. This was like a kid's bedroom. A small kid's bedroom with two very small single beds arranged in a kind of "L" shape. In a couple of places near the window, the walls were streaked with something brown.

I sat on the bed and looked around. It wasn't so bad. If the room stayed cool and I was able to sleep, I could do this. I wished I could smell. The room was in the basement, and I wondered if it was moldy or mildewy.

I took my cooler of food to the tiny fridge. I'd made a bunch of food for a Friday potluck at my permaculture professor's house. I needed to store some and freeze some. I opened the fridge door. It didn't feel very cool, and there wasn't a freezer. Nothing I could do about it now. I crossed my fingers the fridge worked, and I put my food away.

Then I went back to my room and tried the internet. It wasn't working. I wouldn't be able to get any of my school work done here.

I closed the door to the room, stripped down to my skivvies to cool off, and sat on the bed. I felt alone and isolated. I wanted to engage my beginner's mind about all of this, but I just felt miserable and out of place. Why was I doing this? Where did I come up with these ideas, these hare-brained schemes? I felt so tense and teary- and bleary-eyed.

I finally opened up the computer and put in a DVD. I'd brought a couple of movies and some comedy shows. I ate a little bit of Mario's steamed veggies and my quinoa.

After a while I got restless and decided to go to a vegetarian cafe which wasn't far away. I could sit in the air conditioning, order good food, and use their Wi-Fi.

I drove there without getting lost and found a parking spot, which was no easy feat in that area, and then I went into the cafe. They either had no AC or it was broken. It was stifling inside. I stood in the middle of the restaurant looking around. I couldn't stay there either.

I took my computer and went back out and sat at one of the tables along the building. I opened my computer. I needed directions to a few places. I googled those and saved them. Then I sent a few emails.

It was too hot to stay outside. I walked across the street to the Walgreens and went inside. It felt so nice and cool in there.

I couldn't believe I wanted to hang out in a Walgreens.

I drove to Whole Foods next. I was proud of myself for actually finding it since I had no sense of direction in this city. When I was younger, I had been able to find my way almost anywhere. Not anymore. I wondered if all my google mapping had eroded my sense of place. I decided I needed to get a paper map of Seattle so I could figure out where things were.

Yep. That was the answer.

I returned to my little room, turned on the HEPA filter, and ate some dinner. Called Mario. I still felt uncomfortable. I felt hot, fat, ugly. I had gotten my hair cut really short before I left home. I hated it. I looked at myself in the mirror in the bathroom in my little religious house, and I said, "What a pig."

I was so shocked. How could I think such a thing, let alone say it out loud? I immediately apologized to myself and the woman in the mirror.

When I was a girl, my mother had told me that I should look in the mirror and tell myself I was beautiful because a person couldn't count on anyone else to do it.

Guess I wasn't following my mother's advice today.

I had started out so cocky. When I was younger. Smart. Capable. Cute. Now I was unsure of myself, felt awkward and ugly, felt stupid and unaccomplished. This was worse than being a teenager. I hadn't felt ugly then, or stupid or unaccomplished.

Maybe too many years of intermittent depression had warped my brain.

I left the bathroom and went back to my room. It was normal to feel like a stranger in a strange land. I *was* a stranger in a strange land.

I tried to sleep. Couldn't. Finally put the movie *Pride and Prejudice* in the computer and fell asleep to that.

I dreamed I was in the bathroom hugging Anderson Cooper and telling him he needed to get some rest.

Also dreamed some mad man was trying to kill me.

Woke up every half hour or so to pee.

After a while I stopped getting dressed when I woke up. Figured if I ran into anyone on the way to the bathroom, I'd just tell them it was all a bad dream.

In the morning as I was talking to Mario on the phone, I raised my blinds and looked out the half window to the back of the house. Across the tiny alley was a fence. Various bushes or trees grew here and there amongst some rocks. That sweet light of early morning fell in the alleyway. A tiny wren jumped from rock to rock. She stopped and looked at me.

Wrens always reminded me of my friend Linda. She had told me she might come back as a wren.

I watched the wren until I saw a rat just under the fence. He walked from rock to rock, too.

I said to Mario, "There's a rat."

"In your room?"

"No," I said. "I'd already be packing my bags. No, it's about five feet away, outside the window. What's the difference between a rat and a mouse?"

"Pretty much size," he said.

"This is a rat then," I said. "Its tail is about a foot long. And you should see the balls on him. They're huge!"

"That's why there's so many of them," he said.

I laughed.

The rat walked out of my sight line.

I said good bye to my sweetie.

It was time to start this thing.

I drove downtown to the university campus. I parked in shade and hoped it would last. Then I hauled myself and my food inside the campus building and up the stairs. The building felt stuffy and hot.

I found a tiny student lounge with a refrigerator. A woman was in the lounge. She looked past me, like she didn't want to see me. I thought, well, this is a good beginning. I put my food away and looked for the permaculture classroom.

It was hot and stuffy inside that room, too, and the woman I'd seen in the lounge was there. She didn't look up when I came in. The only other person in the room, another woman, looked up, and we said hello to one another.

When the instructor came in, he rearranged the tables so we were sitting more in an octagon than in a large rectangle. The other students began to arrive. Everyone seemed to know everyone else. It hadn't occurred to me that they were probably all going through the same program together, to get their master's degrees. I was there to get a graduate certificate.

I was doing my own lonesome thing. A class of one.

The professor started the class with introductions. We went around the room and talked about ourselves. Everyone seemed so young. And bouncy. Or something. Excited about their schooling and potential new careers?

I had trouble settling down. I felt like such an outsider. The students kept using all these acronyms. "I'm in the C3PO program." "I'm in the ED & X program." I'm making those up, but what they actually said sounded just that alien to me.

When I first started library school many years ago, everyone talked in acronyms or abbreviations, too. It drove me crazy. It felt like a way to keep outsiders from getting access to some kind of secret knowledge. I wanted to set all the abbreviations free and let them live up to their full potential: by becoming whole words.

Anyway, I didn't understand part of the introductions because of the acronyms.

But then we started talking about permaculture.

I first heard about permaculture over a decade ago. The word means permanent agriculture and/or permanent culture. I was intrigued by the idea of mimicking nature.

I was not so thrilled about the idea of having to use farm animals in order to make gardens work. I was not interested in keeping rabbits in cages so I could use their poop. (How could anyone put a rabbit in a cage after seeing them run free in nature?) I didn't find the idea of farming intriguing. I had grown up a farmer's granddaughter, and I knew how difficult and tedious farm work could be—and how lousy the pay.

I loved gardening. But the part I loved was being with the plants and eating their bounty. I hated pulling weeds. It was like Sisyphus pushing that rock up the hill. And I never liked tilling. I worried about the damage I was doing to the soil and the creatures beneath. I didn't like the constant, repetitive and back-breaking parts of gardening.

Permaculture offered relief from all of that.

Recently when I started exploring permaculture again, I saw that permaculture was not a dogmatic set of rules or ideas that I had to "obey" in order to be successful. If I didn't want to cage rabbits or use goat manure or whatever, I didn't need to. The idea was to design with nature. Mimic nature. Design sustainable and efficient food systems and gardening systems that were beautiful and abundant.

Permaculture is all about relationships. It's about people being part of the ecological landscapes. It's about our human landscapes being part of nature.

Permaculture is about social change. It's about visioning and envisioning. About observation. About joy.

The instructor said every design has two clients: the people and the land itself. Permaculture is about turning bad news into good news. All permaculture is different. We learn from mistakes. It's about thinking about what you're doing. Showing up. "It's a reflective process born of observation," the instructor said. "Remember this. Social change takes time. Social change takes no time. Social change is timeless."

We watched a movie with Bill Mollison, one of the fathers of permaculture. He showed where he had practiced the principles of permaculture on his land. It had gone from nearly hardpan to tropical forest in a very short time. He said he worked 30 days over 3 years. After that he could leave for months or more and come back and everything would be fine.

You can't do that with a regular garden. That's one of the differences. The perma in permaculture doesn't mean permanent fields of corn or wheat or soybeans. It's about a permanent, edible forest, filled with perennials. We can eat from it the way animals eat from forests.

With permaculture, the gardens serve many functions. They're habitat, they're full of edibles for us and other creatures, they're beautiful, serene, playful, and they build the soil and clean the air.

In permaculture, you can learn as much from your failures as your successes.

In the movie, Mollison also showed us a hardpan garden in

India. Within a couple of years of using permaculture methods on the land, it was a tropical garden.

After the movie, we talked about relationships in the garden. In nature, plants don't do one thing only. This plant fixes nitrogen *and* provides shade and is edible. This one is beautiful *and* draws insects to pollinate and make honey. This one provides ground cover, repels insects, and is medicinal.

These kinds of partnerships—where the plants provide mutual aid to each other and the garden—are called plant guilds. In his book, *Gaia's Garden: A Guide to Home-Scale Permaculture,* Toby Hemenway describes these guilds as a "group of plants . . . harmoniously interwoven into a pattern of mutual support, often centered around one major species, that benefits humans while creating habitat" (Hemenway 183). The instructor told us how he used permaculture concepts to help a group in Jamaica learn to work together after a longstanding bitterness. I kept thinking about my own work situations where people held onto beliefs that had become outmoded or counterproductive. Could permaculture practices help loosen those kinds of damaging beliefs to reinvigorate work life?

At the lunch break, I offered to drive several people over to the apartment where we were meeting for lunch. As I drove, I looked around and wondered where the trees were. The neighborhoods looked barren in spots, almost like California—as though we were in a hotter, more desert-like climate than in the rainy Pacific Northwest.

My classmates in the car with me hadn't brought any food, so we stopped at a Thai restaurant. They went in to order takeout, and I stayed outside to watch the car.

I was hot and uncomfortable. The air was extremely polluted, and I was coughing. I again wondered what the hell I was doing here. We were supposed to spend the afternoon out of doors. I didn't think that was smart on a 95 degree day when the air was brown.

Eventually we ended up at the house where we were all meeting for lunch. I was so uncomfortable. I didn't feel well. The heat often makes my heart race. I felt dizzy and a bit nauseated. I had gotten heat exhaustion once when I lived in Tucson. Ever since then, my little body just screamed with horror when it got hot. This little house in West Seattle was tiny with no air conditioning.

I wanted to leave. No one talked to me. I didn't talk to anyone. I had to haul all my food up and down stairs. It was all in glass jars so it was heavy. I couldn't keep it in the car because it was too hot, and I needed the food for the potluck later.

We finally drove to the instructor's house, a short distance away. It was 1:30. I had barely eaten or drank anything. I felt dizzy and sick. And freaking hot.

I opened the trunk of the car before we went into the house, to get my inhaler. I dropped my keys in my purse in the trunk.

And then I shut the trunk.

I was four hours from home, and I had just locked my keys in the trunk of my car.

I couldn't believe it.

By now, the stress of the heat and being away from home while I was hungry and dehydrated took over. I went into the house—which was not air-conditioned—and I felt panicked. What was I going to do?

Fortunately the instructor's parents were visiting from Arizona. They gave me their triple A card. We called AAA and they promised to send out a locksmith in an hour or two.

I went out to the deck where everyone else sat listening to the instructor. I didn't have anything to write with. Everything was in my trunk. I didn't have any water. It was in my trunk, too.

Class started.

I don't remember anything about it.

I only remember when I got up to go to the restroom someone took my seat in the shade on the outdoor deck. When I returned, I didn't have anywhere to sit or stand. It was too hot and sunny everywhere.

I just wanted to go home.

Finally, the instructor told us to break up into groups of four and look at the permaculture design and the various systems around the instructor's house. The three people in my group apparently knew one another. They huddled around each other and pointed out things to one another. When I drew near, they walked away. When I said something, they never acknowledged me.

Was this high school?

No, in high school, I was popular.

And not in a bad way. I was friendly with all the different groups.

As we wandered around for an hour, this ostracizing happened again and again.

OK. So I was the new kid. Why try to include me? Why try to make a relationship with me? But wasn't the entire philosophy of this university to build relationships?

Maybe it was me. Maybe I stank. Maybe I seemed aloof.

Maybe they didn't want to be around someone who had so foolishly locked her keys in the trunk.

Maybe they were hot and miserable and only wanted to talk to each other.

Eventually someone came and got me and said the locksmith had arrived. By the time I got up to where the car was, I saw a young man standing next to my car with the trunk open.

I laughed and shouted, "You are my hero!"

He grinned.

CERTIFIED

He asked for my keys. I fetched them from the trunk and gave them to him. Then he leaned over and did some more fiddling. I saw part of a tattoo on his back, near his waist. I was so tempted to lift up his shirt so I could see the rest of it.

"Yep," he said. "When it comes to locks, I'm the magic man. I know I may look like a slacker, but I can do the work."

I said, "Honey, I don't judge people that way. Look at me, I've got white hair and everyone thinks I'm seventy."

He laughed. "Yeah, everyone thinks I'm fifteen, but I'm thirty-two."

He stood up. I smiled and held out my hand. He shook it, firmly.

"What's your name?" I asked.

"Mike," he said.

"Thanks a lot, Mike," I said.

We let go of each other's hands, and he went back to his truck. I waved.

Then I went into the house and hugged the parents of the instructor. What a kind thing they had done for me.

Later I went back down to the bottom of the property to where everyone else was. I had forgotten to get my notebook, so I still couldn't take notes. It was too hot to climb the four stories back to the car. I sat on the grass and tried to listen.

I just wanted to get out of the heat.

I went back inside and watched a movie about permaculture in California.

I slipped on the stairs and nearly fell, but I saved myself.

Score.

We all ate potluck.

I put out my quinoa and black beans.

There was plenty of food. No reason I had hauled all that food all the way from home. Why had I done it? Was I trying to impress them? Make friends? Be part of the group?

No one cared one way or another.

None of the students talked to me as we ate. The instructor asked me a question or two, probably out of politeness. But that was it.

I talked to his parents.

I've always gotten along with older people.

I wondered if no one wanted to talk to me because they thought I was old.

But old people are the most interesting.

I've always thought so.

Probably the other students not talking to me didn't have anything to do with me.

They wanted to talk to each other, not someone they didn't know.

I just wanted to go home.

Right now my home was on the other side of the bridge on the other side of the freeway in the basement of an old house, a few feet from a rat with huge testicles.

I asked someone for directions to get back to the freeway. I listened vaguely. I didn't really care.

I grabbed my stuff, said good bye to the parents, and left. Got in the car and drove. Figured out a way to get out of this part of town and onto the freeway.

Was relieved to be on my own.

I drove to Whole Foods. I got a couple of frozen dinners and a box of cookies.

Then back to my room in the Quaker House. Microwaved one of the dinners. Went into my room and closed the door. Sat in my skivvies cooling off again and eating.

I watched the part of *Pride and Prejudice* I hadn't seen last night. The part where he is walking across the field at sunrise toward her. I love that scene. He's beautiful and vulnerable. It feels so romantic. (And I'm not much of a romantic.)

CERTIFIED

I wondered again why I liked this movie. It often perplexed me. Suddenly I knew why.

I liked it because the man showed up. When he figured out the problem and what he could do about it, he just did it.

That's always been my definition of romantic. I've never liked presents or flowers or candies or any of that stuff. I liked men that truly showed up.

That's what my dad did. He worked at his job. When he was home, he was home for us. He helped us with our homework. He taught us how to do things. He took us places. He was there with us. He showed up.

My husband is the same way. Whenever I see this movie, I think of Mario. Think of how he has shown up every day of our marriage. He isn't a juvenile kind of man and neither is my father. They don't sit around drinking with their friends and whining about their wives like so many men in movies do. Mario and my dad didn't sit around watching TV and not participating in the functioning of the household like so many men in real life do.

Mario shows up. After thirty years, his eyes still light up when he sees me. He still laughs the hardest when I'm funny. He makes spring rolls for me when I've been away. Once when I was gone for a week, he left a half-eaten apple on the table because it reminded him of me (because I was the one who had half-eaten it). He even wrote a poem about it.

I love people who show up. I'm tired of people who have dropped out. Tired of people who want to stay in adolescence.

That was why I liked *Pride and Prejudice*. The two main characters remained true to who they were and they showed up for one another.

I watched the movie to the end and thought of my husband so far away.

I wondered why I was here, alone, instead of at home in bed with him.

Because I was trying to learn to show up better.
To be more effective.
To build better relationships.
Or some thing.

It was tough today being around other people and feeling so alone. But I had done it.

I had trouble sleeping.

I ate the box of cookies.

I showed up for those cookies. They were my best friends in the world.

Science of Joy

I barely slept that Friday night, and I had several nightmares. Someone was stalking people who were doing good works and trying to kill us.

Finally I got up and opened the blinds. No rat. Too bad. I'd been looking forward to seeing him again. The wren was there, though. Or another wren, inches from the window and looking straight at me, tail pointing straight up, looking like half of a "W".

I had a frozen breakfast again. Something about microwaved food always tastes dead to me. We don't have a microwave at home, but I'm glad for them on the road. I figured a couple of days of microwaved food wasn't going to hurt me.

I took the sheets off my bed and cleaned up the room and bathroom. I had decided to leave a night earlier than I'd planned. After class I was driving home to see my sweetie.

I stepped out into another bright sunny day. It wasn't supposed to be as hot as it had been yesterday. I looked at my google map, and then I started my journey to a park near the water where everyone from my Integrative Environmental Science class was supposed to meet. After a couple of blocks, I couldn't follow the map any more: 45th Street was closed. I was stumped. I had no idea which way to go. I pulled off the road and called Mario. He gave me instructions and off I went again.

The road that was supposed to take me through to the park turned into a different road. I drove around a neighborhood. Lost. I couldn't keep calling Mario. He didn't mind, but geez Louise, I felt like a big baby. I promised myself I would get a map of Seattle before the next residency.

Then I pulled off to the side of the road, found my teacher's phone number, and called her. She kept me on the phone and gave me instructions until I saw her in the near distance waving me toward them.

What a sweetie.

The rest of the class, about fifteen of them, stood in the shade of some trees. I parked the car in the bright sun. No trees in the parking lot. The weather people were wrong: I could tell it was going to be a sunny hot day. No clouds in sight.

The park had been a naval base until the seventies. Now the land had many uses with different venues, including several athletic fields and a wetlands project. We were there to explore the wetlands.

Two people from my permaculture class said hello to me. That was a good start. I looked around as we waited. Huge brick buildings to the north of us. (I think it was north.) Must have been barracks. A hangar to the east of us. To the west stretched the various ball fields.

A bunch of us went into the hangar to use their restrooms. We had to walk down a long ugly hallway. Judging from this hallway, it didn't look like the place was in very good shape. I felt like I was one of those guys from *Ghost Hunters* come to explore a haunted insane asylum. Near the bathrooms, a flea market filled a hangar.

Soon enough I was back outdoors. I didn't feel very grounded, so my observation skills were shot. A nice breeze cooled down the day a bit.

Before long, we started our hike. We went around the soccer practice fields where the grass was fake and plastic. I hoped underneath the fake grass wasn't concrete. That would hurt like hell.

Eventually we left the soccer fields behind and went by swales, some with water in them, some nearly dry. Before the base was built, the area had been a peat bog. But the bog had been destroyed long ago. Thousands of years of nature building the peat bog couldn't be replicated—at least not overnight. Instead, they had torn up the concrete and were now trying to build new wetlands. To me, the whole place had an artificial feel to it. But then I grew up at the edge of a marsh in Michigan. This was a new project, and it hadn't had time to fill out.

I admire people who can look at a building, room, or a piece of land and be able to imagine what it could be like. I've never been very good at that. I hoped to develop those skills as I worked on my own designs, starting with the one in my permaculture class.

The class gathered under a small pavilion with bleachers. The gardener for the wetlands and the head of one of the volunteer organizations talked to us about the long process of creating the wetlands.

As they talked, young crows called out from the cottonwoods that surrounded us. I love cottonwood trees. When I was sick many years ago, I used to walk to a cottonwood tree on state property near our house. It was so big I couldn't put my arms all the way around it. I had many long conversations with that cottonwood over the years.

Then the state rented the land out to a rancher, and his cattle trampled the ground all around the tree, muddying the earth and making it difficult to get to the tree. I always wondered if the tree minded. Even now when I go hiking in that area, I stop and say hello to the tree. It's like visiting an old friend.

I saw a hummingbird whizzing here and there beyond the pavilion. On the path to the pavilion from the trail, an adult crow walked, lurching back and forth, reminding me of a bow-legged sheriff. "Hey, partner, new in town?"

The breeze through the trees felt nice. I didn't really care what the speakers were telling us. I just wanted to listen to the trees and birds and watch the interaction of the wildlife around us.

At one point, one of the students (who lived on a reservation near Seattle) told us that to his people, the cottonwood tree "is the tree of life."

He said, "If it falls down, other trees grow up from it. It never dies."

I assumed he was talking about "nurse" logs. When a tree falls and dies in the forest, the log acts as nourishment for saplings to grow up from it. It's remarkable to walk through an old forest and see fifty year old trees growing up from the decomposing body of another tree. A visible testament to the cycle of life.

We eventually went for a walk through the wetlands. The gardener talked. I couldn't hear what she said most of the time because I was near the back of the group. After a while, I didn't care what she was saying. It was hot, and she and the others stood out in the sun. I backed away and found shade whenever I could.

I kept wondering why we were out here on such a hot and sunny day. Shouldn't we have rescheduled this? Wouldn't it be more sustainable not to be so tied to a timetable? Everyone was miserable.

Finally we got off the trail and walked through tall grass. I kept hearing a red-winged blackbird singing. That sound always reminds me of home: A marsh started at the edge of our property out in the country near Brighton, Michigan. When I'd look out into the marsh—or any Michigan marsh—I'd typically see tall blond grasses and cattails, particularly near the transition between forest or field and marsh. And then I'd spot the red-winged blackbirds perched on swaying cattails, like amazingly beautiful black lights, each with a spot of red.

The gardener stopped walking to talk about something—I couldn't hear what—and someone asked about pesticides or "invasive" plants or something. I heard the gardener say they did sometimes use pesticides at the park. I thought, shit, have I been walking around somewhere they've used pesticides? (Later someone told me they'd seen signs warning of pesticide use. I had somehow missed them.)

Chemical pesticides are a line drawn in the sand for me. The damage these chemicals do, along with chemical fertilizers, cannot be underestimated. Last time I checked, 60% of the air in the United States was contaminated with pesticides. Up to 75% of homes may be permanently contaminated with pesticides (partly from termite treatments).

People and pets regularly bring pesticides into homes and buildings, even when the homeowner doesn't use pesticides, just from walking in the neighborhood past homes or lawns where these chemicals are used.

Many pesticides contain neurotoxins. This means they target the nervous system. Pesticides are most damaging to children and pets.

In homes where chemical fertilizers and pesticides are used on the lawns, studies show that animals have dramatically higher incidences of cancer.

I could go on, but the research is so mindlessly depressing.

Knowing what we know, why do people still use them? How did everyone get so hooked on these harmful chemicals?

Over the last thirty years, I've heard every argument (or excuse) for continuing to use them. I haven't been convinced by any of the arguments. If pesticides worked so effectively, they wouldn't have to keep using them.

So when I heard this park gardener trying to justify her use of pesticides, I lost interest in her and the park. I didn't want to be judgmental, but come on. Saying you use a little bit of pesticides is like saying you're a little bit pregnant. Or more accurately, it's like saying, "I'm only going to use a little neurotoxin."

We finally ended up at the edge of a small copse of trees. The gardener let us go into the dark cool center of these woods a few at a time. I was at the end of the group, so I stepped into the shade and semidarkness and stayed for a bit with two other people. A huge root grew above ground from one of the cottonwood trees. It lay on the ground like a downed tree. From this root grew several cottonwood saplings. Just like the man had said. I stood next to this man and his friend, and we marveled at the sight. The root was acting as a nurse tree. The grown cottonwood tree itself looked healthy, growing so close to another cottonwood that they looked like conjoined twins.

For the first time that weekend, I felt connected to the place and to the few people who had stayed behind in the trees with me. I was sorry to leave this little nursery.

After a while, after hours of the heat and the sun and not being able to hear the speaker, I was ready to leave. I had to get my packing done and get out of my room during our hour lunch break.

I left the group a few minutes early and hurried back to the car. I got more directions from Mario. And I got lost several times. I finally ended up on the right road. I found a food co-op and went inside. I was wobbly from the sun and lack of food or water or something—hopefully not from pesticide poisoning—so I went back to my car and just drove to my room.

I got some food and took it into my room where I stripped down again. I was so hot and sweaty. I felt depressed, tired, sad. Alone.

I put on clean clothes, loaded up my car, said goodbye to the place, and headed to school. I got lost. Instead of calling Mario, I just kept driving. Eventually I found the highway. It was packed with cars. It was Saturday. Where was everyone going? I finally made it to school. Parked in the shade and went into the building. It was hot and stuffy inside.

I asked someone at the desk if the AC was still broken. She said, "No, it's just a hot building."

I said, "I didn't sign up for that."

I was paying a lot of money for this experience. I expected the building to be in good working order.

I don't remember much of what we did that afternoon. It was hot. Everyone was uncomfortable. Was this how the world was going to end? Our brains fried from global warming?

We broke up into groups and talked about our experiences at the park. I didn't want to start out this class or these relationships by being critical, and I told the teacher this. I hadn't been thrilled with our jaunt in the park. Since moving out West in 1981, my experience had been that Westerners did not like hearing the truth if it sounded critical or what they called "negative." People generally wanted to pretend everything was great.

How could we make changes for the better if people didn't acknowledge the truth?

The teacher wanted me to tell my truth.

So when it came around for us to talk about our experiences, my group said that the park didn't seem like a true wetland. It was more like a tourist stop. A zoo for wetlands.

And then I mentioned the pesticides.

People around the room began defending the gardener. "She doesn't have enough help so she has to do that." "Maybe she's only using them for a little while." "She's regulated. She has to do it." "She only uses a little bit." On and on.

I was surprised. We were in a program to bring about creative change and to figure out sustainable ways to be in the world; yet most of these students seemed to have swallowed the "we must use pesticides" mantra hook, line, and stinker.

The teacher said, "Look at it from the viewpoint of the people who go to this place. My child sees that sign, and I have to explain what a pesticide is and when she wants to touch the plant, I have to tell her she can't because she might be exposed to a neurotoxin." And a neurotoxin could fry her little brain and nervous system.

I said, "And this isn't about this particular gardener. I've been doing this work for thirty years and I've heard all of this before. What we need to be doing is looking at things from a different perspective. Imagine you are running these wetlands and chemical pesticides didn't even exist, what would you do? Re-envision choices and methods."

The teacher backed me up. It was the first time in decades, maybe ever, that I felt like someone in the know was on my side about the pesticide issue (besides Mario). Most people react about pesticides the same way all the students in the class did. The teacher very adroitly pointed out that there was no "little bit" that rendered pesticides harmless. By their very nature, they are harmful.

We were all supposed to team up to do a semester-long environmental project together. Since I lived so far away, I decided to do it alone. That separated me from the other students again, but trying to coordinate a project like this from two hundred miles away seemed like too much work at this point.

CERTIFIED

I was glad I'd come. I felt like I had an ally in the teacher. But I was ready to go home. While the other students talked about their projects, I left.

I was soon in my car heading for home.

I reflected on the weekend as I drove.

I was surprised how hard it had been. How isolated I'd felt. How strange the city felt.

I was also surprised to find out how much I already knew. Because I've felt like I've failed at so many causes (because I hadn't made any big changes), I figured I must not know very much. Or not enough.

And yet I knew a great deal. I already instinctively tried to garden and live my life in a permaculture way—trying to build relationships and guilds, trying not to cause harm, trying to create sustainable abundance.

I had been viewing myself as a failure for so long that I hadn't been able to see what extraordinary things I have done.

In my novel *The Jigsaw Woman,* the inquisitor says to Keelie at one point, "One day you will be on your knees before me!" Keelie cries, "Never," even though she knows he is right. She keeps standing up. She keeps doing the work. She keeps doing what she thinks is right for the greater good.

I do that. That is my great strength.

I fail and I try again.

I fail and I try again.

Maybe I don't even fail. Maybe it just doesn't work out the way I think it should.

Mario once said to me, "You feel like you're a failure because you haven't won the Nobel peace prize or something." He was exactly right. He just shakes his head. It would never occur to him that he could change the world or do anything so meaningful that someone would give him a Nobel Peace Prize.

When I was nineteen, I was suicidal. In fact, I tried to kill myself. Took a blade and sliced into my arm. Fortunately it hurt, so I didn't cut very deep or very far. The scar is gone now, and I can't remember which arm it was. But I did it because I felt that I hadn't achieved enough. I was nineteen and I hadn't won a Pulitzer.

Plus I was living in a house with several other women who barely spoke to me. It was quite isolating.

Afterward, when I didn't die, I moved into a little attic apartment in Ypsilanti by myself. I went for weeks barely saying a word to anyone, even though I was going to school and working. One night I dreamed a watery nymph (who looked like the actress Carol Kane) came and made love to me. When I woke up, I knew I had started to heal.

I have always had high expectations for myself. I think when you are given much, much is expected. If I am so lucky to have this amazing life, I want to do whatever I can to give back.

Now as I drove away from Seattle, I was satisfied: I had completed my first two residencies, even though it had been extremely physically uncomfortable and emotionally isolating.

I called nearly everyone in my family from the car. I don't usually use the telephone while driving. I did so now with both hands on the wheel and a bud in my ear. I couldn't get a hold of anyone except one brother-in-law. My sister was sleeping, so he and I talked for a long time.

I told him about my permaculture class. We talked about gardening. When he lived in Michigan, he'd made part of his yard into a garden. He remembered years ago when someone in Michigan had made their whole yard into a garden and the neighbors took the man to court because they didn't like it. They all wanted the manicured lawns (which are an English invention—a way for the poor person to emulate the lord's manor). Fortunately the man won the court case and kept his food garden yard.

I told my brother-in-law that if people turned their lawns into food gardens, we could probably end global warming overnight. Do that and overthrow the corporatocracy and we'd be laughing.

I talked about all the social and environmental good food gardens instead of lawns would do, and my brother-in-law agreed but said, "It's just a lot of fun."

I thought, oh yeah, I gotta remember the fun part.

By this time I was about an hour from home. The sun had started to set and the light was golden all around me. I breathed deeply as I looked at the sun on the trees. I was nearing home.

I told my brother-in-law that the battery was almost out on the phone. "I better get going," I said. "I love you."

"You, too, kiddo," he said.

I hung up and turned on the radio. I sang along with some rock 'n' roll song as I drove. I felt peaceful and happy.

Soon I was heading east down the gorge. I grinned when I saw Mount Hood. Home, home, home. The mountain was encircled by pink clouds. For some reason it reminded me of the rings of Saturn.

The road curved, the mountain disappeared from view, the trees grew up on either side of me. I felt joy rising in my bones. I was nearly home. I felt a lump in my throat. I loved the Columbia River Gorge. I loved the huge regal stone faces on the south side of the gorge. I loved Beacon Rock, that inner remnant of a long ago volcano on the north side. It felt like a beacon for home, every time I saw it, resting on the edge of the Columbia River. "This way home, Kim; this way home."

At Cape Horn, above the gorge, the river faded away into the east, with Beacon Rock, the trees, and rock faces all becoming almost blue, like silhouettes in a Japanese painting.

Coming down the hill, I was driving too fast. A sheriff's deputy stopped me. She must have seen I was tired. Or something. I apologized and said, "I'm just coming back from Seattle and trying to get home to my husband."

She let me go with a warning.

And then I was home. There was our little yellow rented house. The daisies were drooping from the heat. The poppies were all closed up. The white morning glories had started twisting up the poppies, choking them. The edges of some of the blue hydrangea blossoms were scorched brown from the heat and sun.

Mario came down the steps with his arms open. We hugged.

I was so glad and grateful to be home.

Late that night, my brother-in-law had a brain bleed. My sister rushed him to the hospital where they immediately did brain surgery.

After I got the news, I kept thinking of my last conversation with him and hoped it would not be my last conversation ever with him. All that I had endured over the weekend—which was fairly minor compared to so many things—seemed trivial. All I cared about now was that my brother-in-law was all right. That my sister was all right.

And I wanted to remember to have fun, to be joyful.

That's what my brother-in-law had said about it all. "It's just fun."

Perhaps that was the best kind of environmental science: the science of joy.

I could learn to be a scientist for joy. When my brother-in-law was well, I'd show him what he had started. That would put a smile on his face.

In-Between

When I first got home from the residency everything felt off-kilter. Was my brother-in-law going to live or die? If he lived, what would his quality of life be like? (I should say this brother-in-law is not legally married to my sister, and she is firm about the fact that they are not married. However, they have been together for at least thirty years. Should I use the word partner? How about I call him Bob?)

So my energy and the energy of my family was focused on Bob and my sister. She had just gotten home after being gone for three months dealing with her own illness, and now this happened. I wanted to do something, anything, but I felt helpless. My stomach was in a knot. I felt jazzed up all the time.

It reminded me of when my dad had his heart problem and then surgery last Christmas. How every second became noticeable. Almost as though I could hear the ticking of a giant clock somewhere. After an hour passed, say, I'd think, "He got through another hour." And my body and mind were frozen, or contracted, with stress and worry, and the stress and worry was exacerbated by the knowledge that stress and worry was not good for me.

I felt it happening all over again. Had felt it in the weeks before my sister got help for her medical condition. This constant waiting for the clock to stop ticking. Or for the other shoe to drop.

So many phone calls between family members. I wished I was there, and I was exhausted by it all. When I was younger, I had wanted to talk about everything, get all our feelings out, figure out family dynamics.

Now it made me tired. I was over it. Done. Crap happened or didn't happen. We inherited crap or didn't inherit crap.

I'd been on overload for so long that I wanted some down time.

And yet wanting that felt selfish in the face of everything that was going on in my family.

I talked with my sisters about what role each of us girls played in our family structure. Five daughters. Sick mother. Father working, often angry. Everyone doing the best they could. I was the one who fixed things, who got things done, who could be counted on.

I had been the one who tried to get to the bottom of things, to the truth of things.

My family relied on me to be the one who stood up. I could be the wall before the fall. The wall to prevent the fall.

Now I was tired.

I couldn't imagine what my sister was going through with Bob. I wouldn't be able to handle it well, I was certain.

Slowly life went on.

For my classes, I was supposed to participate in online discussions between residencies. I was eager for this. I thought I would learn all kinds of wonderful things from my fellow students. I was looking forward to vigorous discussion. I led the first discussion for my permaculture class. Actually, two of us were supposed to lead it. I came up with a bunch of possible

CERTIFIED

discussion topics and my partner helped me wean them down to two topics.

The first topic was: "Many people come out West, particularly to the Pacific Northwest, with the idea of living a self-sufficient or self-reliant life. Some permaculture writers still talk about being self-reliant. Toby Hemenway says that 'self reliance,' as a goal in itself, is a tired old myth that needs to die. It's 'unpermacultural.' What do you think Hemenway means by this? Do you agree or disagree; explain and discuss."

We had some great back and forth on this topic. We talked about the differences between trying (mostly unsuccessfully) to do everything yourself and actively acquiring skills so that you can be a successful participating member of your community.

My second topic was: "Nearly every road in Washington State is sprayed with pesticides, except in Thurston Co. and a few other places. Roadside spraying is ostensibly done to kill weeds that are on the noxious weeds list and to keep roadside flora from obstructing drivers' views. Many counties will allow homeowners to maintain the roadside that bounds their property. Keeping in mind what you've learned about permaculture and the principles of permaculture, how would you maintain the roadside in a way that would satisfy you and the county? Discuss your process. (If you relate more to cityscapes, many cities also spray, particularly sidewalks and public parks. In Bellingham, for instance, they send out crews to spray the cracks in the sidewalks. If this was being done in front of your house/apt. and in your neighborhood, how would you apply permaculture principles?)"

I really wanted an answer to this question. Since I've been working on eliminating pesticides from schools and roadsides for years, I wanted some clues on how to do it better. Plus I thought this was a great question to get them thinking about practical applications of their schooling.

No one answered this question for days. I encouraged some discussion, even if they didn't know the answers. People eventually began talking but most of them seemed ignorant about the ubiquitous use of pesticides. I was shocked. This university was all about getting skills for social and environmental change. How could they not know about pesticide use?

I was flabbergasted, but I was also disappointed. I had eagerly awaited this discussion.

In the weeks that followed, other people led different discussions. I thought the topics were fairly general and simple. "What were your 'ah-ha' moments?" "What do you think about composting?" "What do you think about the cob buildings?" They weren't very challenging questions.

The online site we used to carry on these discussions kept track of how often we posted. (Probably so the instructor could keep track.) By the end of the month, I had posted 37 times. Most people posted about 15 times.

Yikes.

For my permaculture class, we had to do an energy audit and a rainwater catchment analysis on our homes.

I figured out that if we were able to catch all the rainwater from our roof, we'd have 65,000 gallons of extra water! Even if I didn't put in a "formal" gray water system, a rain barrel could help me water my garden. My grandma had a rain barrel right out her back door, and she used it to water all the plants on the porch. (For every inch of rain, you should be able to catch 550 gallons per 1000 square feet of roof.)

I did my energy audit and discovered our major appliances were the main energy sucks. That was no surprise. (Google Scott Russell's "Starting Smart: Calculating Your Energy Appetite," and he'll walk you through it.)

I started my permaculture design for our little rental house and the land it's on. The first thing I did was observe the property: find out where it was shady and sunny, check for any microclimates, etc. Once that was done, I measured every part of the property and then drew it on a paper grid with colored pencils. This was the "before" permaculture map.

I had never done landscape drawing. I didn't know how to do landscape drawing. I thought, "OK, I'm taking this class to learn how to do permaculture, but I'm learning most of this stuff on my own. Wasn't I paying a lot of money to sit here trying to figure out these kinds of things on my own?"

I did the drawing, but I was nervous about it. I wasn't an artist. I knew at least one person in the class was an architect. I couldn't compete with that.

Of course, we weren't competing. This school was all about collaborating. Eventually we would show each other our individual plans to be inspired by each other, to get ideas from each other, and to offer constructive criticism.

During this month, I became aware of my complete inability to relax. One of my sisters told me not long ago that I had to be the best at everything. I said, "That isn't true because I am *not* the best at everything." But I realized now, during this month, that she was right.

I had spent a lot of time figuring out the "perfect" discussion questions. I got online frequently, as we were encouraged to do, to respond to my fellow students. I did my energy audit and rain catchment calculations and posted them first. I thought about the questions my environmental science teacher posted for us and gave detailed, thoughtful answers.

I wanted to do well. I wanted to be the best. Unconsciously. Once I was conscious of this desire, I tried to mitigate it. This wasn't about some teacher thinking I was great. It wasn't about a group of students thinking I was great. I was trying to *learn* something. To learn many somethings.

Mostly what I was learning was that I knew a great deal

already. I already knew most of the material I was reading for the integrative environmental science class. Integrative environmental science is about how humans affect the environment and how the environment affects humans.

I've been doing environmental work since I was a girl in elementary school trying to prevent boys from destroying killdeer eggs. I knew what was happening to our biosphere because of humans. As I read chapter after chapter about the harm we were doing to the planet, I could feel myself becoming more and more depressed. I knew this stuff. I didn't need to hear it again. I wished everyone knew about what was happening to the planet.

Because once they knew, they'd change, right?

Because what you realize—once you understand the science of the various interconnecting ecological systems—is that it is possible for all of these systems to bounce back. Presently, if we changed our ways—and most of the time the changes are so exciting and marvelous—Nature will heal itself. These systems still have resiliency. But soon, as far as some of these systems are concerned, resiliency will be lost. They won't be able to bounce back. We won't be able to bounce back.

Think about yourself. Think about how different you are when you are relaxed and healthy. Now imagine yourself stressed and overloaded. It's easier to bounce back from obstacles if you started out relaxed and healthy.

All in all, it was a stressful month, and I was glad when it was over.

Inflexible Me, Part 1

August

I left Thursday morning for my second residency in Seattle. Mario was in Vancouver for union negotiations, so I didn't get to see him. The day was cool and overcast: perfect driving weather. When I got close to Seattle, the drivers became more aggressive. Everyone was driving too fast. When I signaled and then changed lanes, well ahead of any other car, the drivers invariably honked and flashed their lights at me, as though I had done something wrong.

Earlier in the year when I was driving in the Los Angeles area and complaining about the drivers, my friend Jenine (who is from California) told me that generally speaking California drivers know what they are doing. Once I accepted this, I stopped panicking every time someone swerved in front of me or drove too close to me. Driving in the Los Angeles area became much easier after that.

Seattle drivers must have their own logic and way of doing things, too. But I was a stranger and didn't understand it. Every time I asked someone who lived in Seattle about the traffic, they were not reassuring. They invariably agreed that it was crazy. Then they'd start telling me their Seattle-driving horror stories.

I arrived at the Quaker apartments and got the key to my room. This time I was assigned the smaller room with a double bed. I liked it. It felt more like a bedroom or a hotel room. A painting of irises and violets hung on the south wall, and a painting of a fritillaria hung on the west wall. Right next to the bed was a painting of mountains with their reflection in a glacier pond. It was called *Wilderness*.

I felt quite welcomed in this room. I opened the shade and looked out the window at the alley and wondered if my wildlife friends from my previous residency were there.

I didn't see him (the rat) or her (the wren).

I was worn out and stressed out from the drive. I wondered again if I could keep doing this for a whole year. I ate some quinoa and vegetables I'd brought.

Before it got too late, I decided to drive to Lakeview Cemetery. I had heard somewhere that walking in this cemetery was like walking in a forest, only this forest had graves scattered here and there. I looked at my Seattle city map and thought I figured out where it was, and then I drove toward it.

I got lost twice. I still had no sense of direction when it came to Seattle.

Eventually, I found the cemetery and turned into the drive.

It looked like every other cemetery in the United State. The forest cemetery I had heard about must have been somewhere else. I didn't even get out of the car.

Next to the cemetery was Volunteer Park. I stopped there and walked around. On the side near the cemetery, kids played in a fountain while their parents watched. I walked away from the cemetery into a kind of rolling lawn with huge old trees growing here and there. Their bark and coloring reminded me of cedar trees, only these trunks were huge and the branches swooped down to the ground so that from far away each looked like a tall pointed tent (slightly off the ground). Up close and underneath, it was like a tree-made fort or cave. Or like the swooped branches were arms holding up green frockery as they danced, as they danced, as they danced.

Lots of images came to me as I oohed and aahed over the trees.

I felt almost peaceful, almost grounded, standing next to these very old trees.

Oooh.

Ahhh.

Later I drove to Whole Foods and got a frozen dinner and some cookies. Went back to my room, ate, watched DVDs, got a few hours of sleep.

Woke up to gray skies and a bit of cloud sweat. So much nicer than it had been last residency. Had I become so acclimated to the Pacific Northwest that I preferred cloudy days?

Sometimes.

Made it to school easy as pie this time. Parked on the side of the building on Battery, by the car wash. A huge sign of a happy pink elephant spraying itself with neon water slowly turned next to the car wash. I paid too much for parking and went into the school building and up to the class.

I didn't feel like I was as much of a stranger this time around. I did feel a little dizzy, though, so I asked if we could turn off the fluorescent lights. That helped. I got a little steadier. We went around the room to check-in.

When it was my turn, I told them that over the last month I had discovered I liked to have a how-to list when I was learning something new. I had felt a bit at sea trying to learn so much of this stuff on my own by trial and error.

Later the instructor said it was important to understand that permaculture wasn't about doing something step by step. We had to rely on our intuition and trial and error.

On the face of it, that was great advice. I would love to learn everything by using my intuition. But we all learn differently. Some by reading, some by hearing, some by doing. For some things, I actually want blow-by-blow instructions. I have often gotten frustrated watching various men in my family taking too long (in my mind) getting projects completed because they hadn't read the directions on something they were installing.

I read directions. I methodically figure out how to fix problems. I'm the one in our family who puts together the tangle of satellite, DVD player, VCR, and television wires and cables so that we can watch TV.

When I was a kid, I liked taking clocks apart.

Then I'd put them back together.

I didn't have instructions then. I just did it.

Had I lost the ability to just do things instinctively, relying on my own know-how?

Or do we sometimes just need instructions?

After check-in, we talked about our permaculture projects. Then we all taped our "before" maps to the wall in the classroom and walked around and looked at everyone else's maps.

The plans were interesting, but I didn't learn a lot by looking at them.

I kept wondering if I was missing something. Some piece of it all. Everyone else seemed so engaged, and I still felt separate.

After we looked at our maps, we watched a movie. It was a movie about permaculture that I could get off YouTube. Why was I wasting time watching a movie in class? A twenty year old movie at that. I only saw this instructor and these people in real life three times a term. I wanted to have a discussion or brain storm. Something. I did not want to sit in class watching a movie.

CERTIFIED

I had to get my mind right. I couldn't spend the next year criticizing everything that happened in the classroom.

I remembered what the director had told me when I was considering attending this school: The instructors were "guides on the side" not "sages on the stage."

Was I so accustomed to the "sages on the stage" way of education that I just couldn't get into the swing of the "guides on the side?"

We broke for lunch. I heard everyone arranging rides to our next destination, the Medicinal Herb Garden at the University of Washington. I didn't pay any attention. I quickly got my map from the wall and left.

The Quaker house was near the University of Washington, so I figured I'd go to the house, have lunch, and then meet the others at the herb garden after I ate. The instructor had told us we could park on the street at the university. I had emailed him earlier in the week, letting him know that I needed directions so I could make a google map. He told me he'd give us directions. He added, "I haven't lost anyone yet."

I still wanted the directions. I listened to his directions in the classroom and hadn't understood them one bit. I didn't think he understood that I really did not know the city.

In my room, I ate a quick lunch. Then I looked at the map on my computer again and again, so that I clearly knew where I was going. When I was fairly certain I knew where I was going, I headed out.

I got lost almost immediately. The road I was supposed to turn down wasn't there. Or didn't have a sign. Or something. And there was absolutely no street parking. What had the instructor been talking about? I had to stop and ask directions twice. I got a map of the campus. I still couldn't figure out where I was.

Finally I put the car in a parking structure, and I walked onto campus. The air was humid and still smoky from fires burning around Washington. My breathing became a little ragged as I walked down the sidewalk, past the chemistry building on one side and greenhouses on the other. I wondered if I should go to the greenhouses to see if my group was there, but then I saw what I supposed was the Medicinal Herb Garden.

I walked up under the trees and into the herb gardens. I saw raised bed after raised bed of plants. I saw pink petals blown back from the burnt orange center of echinacea plants and the round prickly balls of a milk thistle and I figured I was in the right place.

Only no one else was there.

I walked up and down the seven large sections of the gardens, from one end to another, several times. No one else came.

I heard jets overheard. I looked up. The Blue Angels flew over. I walked the gardens looking for my classmates. Maybe I was early. Maybe they had all gotten trapped in traffic. Wasn't I special getting there on time?

I stopped and asked a couple of people if this was the medicinal herb garden.

The man said, "No, it's over there." He pointed.

"By the greenhouses?"

"Yep."

"Are you sure?" the woman asked. "These look like medicinal plants."

I walked across the street, toward the greenhouses. I didn't see any of my classmates. In fact, I didn't see any other people. I did notice the sign for the Medicinal Herb Garden: across the street where I'd just been.

I went back to the herb gardens. I sat on a bench and tried to look around. Tried to relax. So what if I missed the class? I was here in the gardens. I should just enjoy it.

But I couldn't relax. Couldn't enjoy it.

The Blue Angels kept thundering overhead. Exploding

overhead. The sound was so loud I had to cover my ears—and I already had cotton in them. Soon every time the jets screamed overhead, I dropped my notebook, covered my ears, and screamed at the top of my lungs.

No one heard me.

For one thing, no one was around.

No classmates.

When I'd been there for about half an hour. I walked over to the greenhouses. Just then an unfamiliar man came walking outside, followed by my classmates.

They'd been there all along? I'd been in the wrong place?

I was so angry I could hardly stand it.

I guess I had misheard the instructions.

Or misread them.

Or something.

How stupid could I have been to go to the wrong place?

And the instructor acted as though it was no big thing. Who cared that everyone had been waiting or lost or whatever? Let's just carry on.

I was mortified.

Now I was some batty old lady who kept getting lost.

I tried to listen to the man talk about the garden.

But I just felt myself drifting further and further away.

Why was I doing this? Why was I here? What was I learning looking at this garden?

I floated from here to there.

An hour and a half later, we were instructed to go to the next rendezvous spot. We had fifteen minutes to get to a house that was about twenty minutes away.

I trekked to my car, alone, got back on the road and immediately got lost again. I called Mario, but what could he do? I finally said I was going to have to figure it out one way or another. The maps weren't working. The traffic was bad.

I kept telling myself it didn't matter. If I didn't get there on time, it did. not. matter.

None of this was important enough for me to be so stressed out.

I got to the right street, and I saw all my classmates walking down the road. I waved. I was in the right place.

The teacher had instructed us to park far from the house, so we wouldn't block the drive or bother any of the neighbors. I parked the car and walked down the street where I'd seen everyone.

All of my classmates were gone. I looked up and down the street.

Nothing and no one. Just suburban quiet. My classmates had apparently disappeared into thin air.

I had the address though. I opened my notebook and looked it up. There. On that mailbox. I walked up to the door to the house near the mailbox. I knocked. I rang the bell. I called out.

No one answered.

It was a dumpy house. I thought it was strange we were going here. Someone was home though. The back of their car was open with groceries in the back. I saw a dog next door. I didn't want to deal with a dog.

Where was everyone?

I called and called.

I walked down the stairs to the large back yard.

No one.

I saw a stream in the back yard. A glimpse of it between the trees. Dark running water.

I wanted to be there.

I started back to the road. I was exhausted. I couldn't believe this had happened again.

I started to cry. Only the tears didn't come.

All dried up.

CERTIFIED

I was going home.

Fuck. This. Shit.

I pulled myself up the stairs and walked back to the road.

One of my classmates was standing across the street looking up and down the road.

She saw me and said, "I thought you might not know where we were."

Instead of being grateful, I was once again furious.

"I can't believe I have gotten left behind twice today," I said. And then I swore. Or something. Said I was going home. She said, "But it's really nice in there."

So I went in.

The whole class was crowded around a cistern in the middle of a cluttered yard.

The owners talked enthusiastically about their garden, their water system, their solar panels, their bees. Their bees' knees.

All things I was interested in.

Or had been.

I wasn't any longer.

I just wanted to leave.

I thanked the young woman who had come to get me.

Later one or two people tried to talk to me. But I floated away. I didn't care. I didn't matter to them, so they didn't matter to me.

I wasn't part of their little group.

Of course I wasn't. At this university, they worked in cohorts. They all knew each other from the beginning of the program to the end. I was not part of their cohort. I wasn't part of their own little college clique.

I wondered if this was how people had felt in high school when they weren't part of a particular group.

I hadn't paid any attention to cliques when I was in high school. I was so great and wonderful I just figured everyone would want to know me and be with me. The whole world was my clique.

That's what I say now, but I was anorexic-bulimic the summer before I started high school. I was scared to death of it.

Fast forward a few decades.

Quite a few.

While we were at this house looking at everything the owners had done to try to lessen their carbon footprint, I tried to force myself to engage in the experience. I couldn't seem to do it. I knew this was one of the hallmarks of depression, but I didn't feel depressed. I felt disengaged.

Perhaps my brain had been so damaged by depression and stress that I had become inflexible. I could no longer roll with the punches. Or whatever that expression was.

I felt no affection for anyone. No empathy.

I wanted to leave.

When no one was looking, that's what I did.

I got in my car and drove back to my room.

I called Mario. I wanted to curl up into a ball. I wanted to go home. I wanted to quit.

Why was I doing this?

Really. Why?

Because I hadn't sold a novel in a while.

Because I wanted to contribute something to my world.

Because I had to make a living.

Why couldn't my writing be enough?

I had gone on a visual meditation recently (a journey). And my guides in the meditation said I was too scattered. I needed to figure out what I was good at and do that one thing. If everyone in the world did that, wow! What a world we'd have.

At the time, I argued with them. My one thing was writing. But a girl's gotta make a living.

Was this schooling going to help me make a living? How?

CERTIFIED

Get a job at a nonprofit making shit wages while working my ass off and getting sick from the stress or from some crappy building I was working in. No. I'd done that, been there.

I didn't want to do it again.

So why was I doing this?

I called a friend who lives in Seattle. She's also a writer. She feels like an old friend, and we understand each other's worlds. Sometimes that is so necessary: To be around people where you don't have to explain or justify yourself.

She said she'd come get me. I didn't have to drive anywhere.

Oh my.

And she did come get me. She took me to the Fremont Troll. We drove up under the Aurora Bridge, on Troll Avenue, and there at the end of the road was a gigantic troll made out of concrete.

We parked the car and walked over to the troll. Its one eye was shiny (made from a hubcap, apparently). In its left hand, it crushed a Volkswagen bug. Three men sat about twenty feet in front of the troll, playing guitars and singing. Other people clambered up onto the troll.

I said hello to the troll and thanked it for letting me visit this burg.

We headed out again. It was so relaxing being in the passenger's seat. We ended up at a park looking out at Puget Sound.

The sun was beginning to set, and the sky was pink. I walked with my friend to the water's edge and looked out across the bay. The water lapped against a beach that was made of stones and seashells.

Seashells.

Yes, I felt the Old Mermaids here.

I breathed in the sound of the Old Sea.

I felt like myself again.

My friend and I talked of many things as the sun went down.

And then it was time to leave.

What a needed respite our few hours together had been.

I went back to my room with visions of the Troll in my head.

I decided not to quit school.

I could do it for one more day.

Inflexible Me, Part 2

I read a little before I went to sleep. Joan Didion's book *The Year of Magical Thinking* was on the shelf. I flipped through it. I knew it was about when her husband died suddenly. My heart was in my throat as I read paragraphs here and there.

How does one handle such tragedies?

I didn't want to think about anything happening to my husband. He was my closest friend. The only one on the planet who loved me truly. I would be absolutely bereft if anything happened to him.

My father had been married to my mother for fifty-two years, and then she got what they thought was a cold. Six hours later she was dead.

Shit.

Life was so difficult sometimes.

I don't remember what I dreamed that night.

I had wanted to get up early and return to the Medicinal Herb Garden. I woke up on time, but the thought of trying to find the garden again and a place to park seemed monumental. I called Mario, and he told me I'd gotten an email. My youngest sister's mother-in-law had gotten suddenly ill and was in the hospital with pneumonia and septic shock.

That's what had happened to my mother. Six hours later and she was dead.

But this woman was just a few years older than I was. She would be all right.

I'd call my sister later. I sat on the bed and did some Reiki for her.

Then I got dressed and drove to school.

Once we were all gathered, we did a check-in. I complained about the traffic. I was sure this was getting tiresome. I told my classmates about becoming lost twice the day before and getting left behind. How I had wanted to quit, but I decided to come here today. I said I was so glad we were not leaving the classroom. The teacher said they'd all wait on me today, bring me whatever I wanted.

Then we talked about how the month had gone. Some people complained about long posts on our online system. About how they felt overwhelmed when they went to a thread, and they saw "like 500 words" and they didn't know what to do. Others nodded in agreement.

My jaw fell to the floor. I'm sure of it. I picked it up and closed my mouth.

500 words was too much for them to comprehend?

I was a freaking novelist. And these people couldn't read 500 words? What did that say about my particular skill, my particular passion?

Had the world of tweets and twits and whatever changed our brains or our habits so that we couldn't read any more than a few sentences without getting bored or losing comprehension?

I could barely breathe thinking about the consequences of this.

CERTIFIED

But I switched back to student mode. I couldn't think about publishing houses crashing and burning because people couldn't read any more. I couldn't think about all the stories that wouldn't be written because writers couldn't make livings.

A big part of our learning for these courses is our online discussions. I had not been impressed with the discussions thus far. We had been admonished not to write too much or too little. Now people were complaining about people writing too much.

I was the only one who had written more than a paragraph or two.

So they were complaining about me.

One woman who was in my online discussion group went on and on about people writing too much.

We had five people in our group. Three of them hadn't posted anything in a week.

She was talking about me.

So I said, "How can you have a meaningful conversation one line at a time? I don't know how to say anything of import in one or two sentences."

I don't roll that way, peeps.

I felt a wee bit attacked.

I'm not saying I was being attacked. I just felt that way.

And I felt out of step.

But I didn't feel like I was wrong about this issue.

I had spent twenty years in illness. Twenty years that should have been my juiciest, when I should have been out in the world making my way, my name, my living.

All gone.

And now I was here trying to do this. Twenty years too late.

They didn't want a novelist. They wanted a twit. Ter.

Later we broke up into our new online groups. I felt myself detaching. I just didn't belong to these people.

And yet I'd paid money. I'd borrowed money. I owed money. I'd paid my time. I had to try harder.

I needed to engage.

So I listened to them. Talked with them. They were all young enough to be my children.

They saw me as an old woman.

With nothing to say or contribute.

Bullshit. I didn't know what they thought. They didn't know what I thought.

We had a panel discussion next. The teacher had gathered five community leaders to talk about how they had accomplished change. Everything took time, they said. They had to persevere. They had to navigate through bureaucracies that did not want to change. They had to find allies in these bureaucracies.

I thought about my own environmental and social justice battles (and they all felt like battles). It had always taken so much time. It had been difficult to persevere.

Perhaps we were losing the ability to be resilient, to keep trying even when people kept turning us away.

It took a particular kind of person to do this kind of work, and yet, we needed to do it.

They talked about how most people want the same thing: They want to live in communities that are safe and where their families can be happy and healthy. It's important to find the leverage point. Ideally, as I understand it, a leverage point in a system is that place or point where you can push for change with the least amount of effort for the greatest impact.

I listened, fascinated. All of the people on the panel had created organizations or environmental projects within the city of Seattle. I wondered if it was easier working on environmental change in a city. I wished someone on the panel had done some work in rural areas.

CERTIFIED

When we broke for lunch, I walked to Whole Foods with one of my classmates. She was about my age and lived on a reservation not far from Seattle. We walked in the rain. She mentioned that this panel was the best she had seen since she'd come to the university.

I had never been to this Whole Foods, and it was huge. While my classmate walked around, I went outside to check my phone messages. I had a message that my youngest sister's mother-in-law had died.

She was barely sixty years old. Dead. Out of the blue.

Just like my mother. Only this woman was twenty years younger than my mother had been.

I stood in the rain feeling paralyzed. How does shit like this keep happening?

This year had just been filled with one mindless awful thing happening after another.

Last month when I'd been in Seattle for my classes, my sister's partner had a brain bleed and they had thought he was going to die. Now my other sister's mother-in-law had died.

Our family had had a rough year: my father's heart problems, hospitalization, near death on the operating table, and recovery. My sister's illness and three month stay at a recovery facility. My sister's partner's brain bleed last month. And now this.

I stood in the rain trying to comprehend this awful thing. Stood in the rain shivering. If something like this could happen to a woman close to my age, it could happen to me.

I called my youngest sister. Left a message of condolence.

Soon enough I was walking back to school with two of my classmates. I told them what happened.

I said, "It's so awful for them. And then part of me thinks, this could happen to me."

The other woman said, "Don't draw that to yourself."

I said, "I don't believe in that New Age bullshit."

Ah, yes, Kim: How to win friends and influence people.

She looked at me and said very firmly, "That's what my people believe."

Oh shit. I'd forgotten she was Oneida.

"The grandfather tells the story of the two wolves," she said. Quickly, almost angrily. (What an ass I am, I thought.) I nodded. I knew this story. "The boy wants to know which wolf will win. The grandfather says, 'whichever one you feed.'"

We crossed the street and walked between buildings as the cloud sweat fell on us.

"Yes, yes," I said. "I see that."

"You're so dynamic and charismatic," she said. "You have such presence. But—"

Ah yes. As long as I could remember, people have felt like they could tell me what was really wrong with me. Truly. Sometimes strangers. Sometimes friends. "You'd be pretty if only you did this that or the other." "People would get along with you better if you did this that or the other." "You are so this that or the other, but—"

She didn't finish her sentence. Or if she did it was lost in the sound of traffic.

I would be so great if . . . I wasn't like how I am.

But I knew what she meant. I so easily got caught up in what was going wrong in my life. Like a fish who kept struggling on the hook and making it just go in deeper.

We got back to school. They went inside. I went around the building and called Mario and told him the news. Then I leaned against the building, facing the turning pink elephant by the car wash, and I wept.

For the second half of the day, we broke into our groups again and gave presentations to each other. Someone in our group

CERTIFIED

showed a video about how mushrooms can save the world. It was fascinating. Fungi are the oldest species on the planet, and we're more closely related to fungi than to anything else, according to Paul Stamets, mycologist extraordinaire. Fungi have so many amazing properties. They can be used for bioremediation, as natural pesticides and antibiotics. According to Stamets, fungi can save the world. (You can find his video "6 Ways Mushrooms Can Save the Planet" on YouTube.)

Other people talked about green roofs, better energy use, and city canopies. I talked about the jaguar and the deleterious effect the problems at the border may be having on its comeback in the Southwestern United States. The jaguar is considered an apex and a keystone predator: It is at the top of its food chain. These types of predators activate what conservation biologists call a trophic cascade. Their predation of other predators causes other species to thrive.

Here's an example. When the gray wolf was released into Yellowstone, they killed elk. Less elk along the riverbanks allowed riparian trees and bushes to come back. These floras then cooled the water which allowed fish species to return.

Isn't that something?

I enjoyed these presentations.

They broke into their project groups after this, so I left early. It had been a great day and an awful day.

I found my way easily onto I-5 in the rain. I started home.

I don't remember what I thought about. I ate another box of Pamela's cookies.

Gotta stop doing that.

I understood completely why people did drugs. Why they drank. I ate. I wanted to learn better ways to cope.

At Olympia, I stopped at the co-op and bought more cookies. I sat in the car and ate quinoa and vegetables. Healthy stuff. Then I spoiled it all by eating cookies.

I never used to eat sweets.

Got on the road again. Thought about the weekend. Thought about my life. I still didn't understand how and why this was so difficult for me.

Why couldn't I be easygoing?

Maybe it was all too late. This was who I was. Celebrate it and move on.

So many people had experienced so many horrific things in their lives, and they bounced back. They made successes of their lives.

I had been ill for a couple of decades. I am still ill. Still struggle. And I am still angry about it. Still don't understand it. Still don't know why I am not completely well.

Still.

I kept using that word.

Maybe I needed to keep still for a while.

Or build a still.

One of my great grandfathers had been a bootlegger, after all.

By the time I got to the gorge, it was almost dark. The trees on either side of the road that went along the river looked different. Preternatural. As though I had turned into some other world.

Maybe I was altered from the sugar. From the stress. Exhaustion. Grief.

I didn't know. I felt like I was floating. And the trees were there, a part of it all, a part of me. Silver and green as twilight fell.

I kept driving as dark descended. Usually at this time of night, I didn't like to drive. I can't see very well. Impending doom waits to fall. I look for deer around every corner.

But something changed.

I felt as though I was in a cocoon.

Nothing was going to happen to me. And even if it did, oh well.

I rested my elbow against the door and window and leaned my head against my hand as I drove.

I knew this wasn't a good idea. I might fall asleep.

But I knew I wouldn't.

Perhaps the faeries were guiding me home.

Or the Troll.

Maybe my car was possessed.

I can't describe it. It just felt very odd and peaceful.

Nearly transformative.

I followed the curves of my beloved River and Gorge until I reached my beloved human.

He ran out of the house and down the stairs to greet me. He wrapped his arms around me.

Home, home, home.

I needed nothing else.

At least not now.

The next day, Mario took the car in for an oil change. They found a bat on our grill. They'd never seen anything like it. I asked Mario, "Was it beautiful? Was it sad? Was it disgusting?"

"It was all of those things."

Kind of like me.

Something about this discovery sent chills through me. As though this was an explanation for something.

I remembered bats symbolized birth, death, and rebirth. Especially a shamanic death. (Of course, the bat was a living being that was now dead. Nothing symbolic about that.)

Had the spirit of that bat carried me safely home?

I went outside and looked at the car. A spot of maroon-colored blood stained the grill.

I said a little prayer to the bat. Thanked it for its sacrifice.

Now what?

I'd figure out a way to honor it, and all those souls that have gone before me.

One way or another.

Jewelweed

September

During the month between residencies, I finished up *Jewelweed Station,* a novel I had been working on since late winter. It felt great doing something I loved, being comfortable with it, having fun with the story. I fell in love with writing again—or else I let the disappointment of my publishing experiences evaporate, and I could see that I still loved writing.

I also worked on my master plan for the permaculture class and my final project for integrative environmental science.

First I mapped my house and property the way it is now. (We rent.) For the master plan—or the "poof!" plan as the instructor called it—I needed to permaculture our house and property (at least on paper). Incorporating much of what I'd learned all term, I let my imagination soar.

First I put in a rain catchment system to harvest my rainwater. I calculated that if I caught all the water from my roof, I'd get 68,000 gallons in a year. Wow. (Even someone in the desert can harvest quite a lot of water from their roof.) Even without filtering or cleaning the rainwater from the roof, I could use the rainwater to water much of my garden, particularly the perennials (where I don't eat the leaves), and to flush the toilets (about 10,000 times).

I also put two solar panels on the front of the house, plus a solar water heater. In most houses, water heaters use a lot of energy, so a solar water heater would save us lots of money (besides helping to reduce overall energy use).

Mostly my poof! plan had lots and lots of food. What I've learned about permaculture (and about ecological gardens in general) is that we have the potential for amazing abundance in our own backyards, no matter how tiny or unproductive they seem to be. I live on a small lot, yet I was able to design for apple, walnut, and cherry trees. (We've already got several prune plum trees.) I also designed for mulberry and blueberry bushes, plus espaliers of apples, pears, and berries. I planted maple trees for shade, and lots and lots of wildflowers because I love them, and because they're good for the birds and butterflies. I put in a huge vegetable garden, and I made room to "grow" worms.

In permaculture, we design for diversity, and everything has multiple uses. For instance, daikon radishes break up the soil, and they're edible. An apple tree provides shade, flowers for the bees and butterflies, and fruit for people and animals. Some plants fix nitrogen and provide food. Other plants are beautiful for us to look at, and they provide habitat for the birds and the bees. And on and on.

My before-permaculture drawing showed a sweet-looking, but rather barren landscape. The after-drawing, the permaculture poof! plan, was so filled with color and life—so much abundance.

The most important thing the permaculture class taught me was just that: The possibility for abundance is everywhere. We need to do the initial work and then within eighteen months, more or less, we're not thinking about what we don't have but about what we're going to do with all the abundance.

For my integrative environmental science project, I had planned on designing an ecological garden for the community library. For the final presentation, I decided that each of my fellow students would play the part of a community member while I advocated for a permaculture garden around the library. I wrote little (compassionate) biographies of people in town who help out with the library, and I assigned a name to each student randomly.

Most of the students live in an urban area and don't do any work in rural areas. I wanted to give them an opportunity to walk in someone else's shoes and see what their reactions might be to this proposed change.

I finished both projects well before I was due to leave for Seattle.

Our car was acting up, so I decided to rent a car to go to Seattle. Not only would I be spared the worry of breaking down, I'd have use of a CD player, and I could listen to a book on audio. I was hoping that would help make the drive up to Seattle more tolerable.

And I was right. The drive to Seattle was event-less. No rude drivers. No traffic jams. I listened to the second half of *Manhunt*, the true life story of the hunt for John Wilkes Booth after he murdered President Lincoln. (I'd listened to the first half while driving from Phoenix to Santa Barbara in February.)

I was almost in Seattle when the car went over a patch of bumpy pavement, and I had a bout of vertigo. I was immediately nauseated and terrified. I realized then that the car had been "wobbly" the whole ride, and it had made me a little car sick.

I got to "home" in Seattle, my little room in the Quaker House. Unfortunately the key they'd left for me didn't work. I could get into my room, but I couldn't lock it. It took me a while to convince the young woman on the other end of the phone that being able to lock my room was important for me. Eventually she seemed to understand; she arranged to get me a key, and all was well in my little world.

I was still feeling sick and dizzy, so I drove to campus (University of Washington), parked my car, and walked to the Medicinal Herb Garden. Last time I'd been here, I was lost, waiting impatiently for my classmates only to discover I'd gone to the wrong meeting place. This time I walked slowly around the garden, looking at the flowers and plants, trying to ground myself and feel better.

After a few minutes, I walked over to a huge old cedar tree. I rested my cheek against it, then sat on a bench beneath it, meditating. I felt as though I was sitting near Yggdrasil, the World Tree. I breathed in and out, in and out. I could hear the buses running outside the garden, saw students walking on the paths around the gardens, and I breathed and tried to relax.

After a while, I got up and walked toward a small orange flower. It turned out to be jewelweed, a plant I'd never seen but had starred in the novel I'd just finished.

In the novel, Callie notices one lone jewelweed growing by her mother's grave: "Jewelweed. Usually it grew closer to the water and was surrounded by other jewelweed. It was one of her mother's favorite flowers. Her mother said people often didn't see jewelweed or ignored it if they did see it, even though it was a great healer. Get stung by nettle or touched by poison oak and the juice from jewelweed would sooth the inflammation away. Her mother believed wildflowers could fix anything."

It was nice to see this plant here and now. I started to walk away. I turned, and everything in the background became blurry, as though I had moved too quickly for my vision to keep up. This had happened before, usually when I was tired, but just then I felt a little afraid and vulnerable. Was something happening to my vision? I turned quickly again to try and recreate the effect.

It didn't happen again.

I told myself to calm down. Maybe it wasn't anything physical. Maybe something energetic was happening in the garden. I walked to the other end of the bed, to see what was growing with the jewelweed.

I had to laugh: It was black cohosh.

I didn't know a lot about black cohosh, but I recalled it was considered to be a powerful "women's herb." I decided to sit next to it and meditate on it. Immediately I "saw" a powerful witch-like Kali-like figure. She was dark purple and full of motion. She had lots of advice for me. Mostly I knew I could call on her to fill me up with courage. (In *Jewelweed Station,* my main character, Callie Carter, pretends she is docile and compliant. When she has difficulty pretending, she fills herself up with the spirit of jewelweed. This gives her the courage to hide and protect herself, to gather information and power, until the time is right to reveal herself.)

I thanked the plants and trees. Then I drove to Whole Foods to get dinner. I returned to my place, watched two Netflix DVDs of *Entourage,* then fell asleep. I thought of black cohosh before I drifted asleep.

I dreamed someone phoned me, and the person sounded just like my mother. I was so excited to hear her voice. But as I talked with this person, I realized it wasn't her, and that made me very sad. In another dream, I was talking to my boss about a dream I'd had about him. He had huge white teeth in the dream. He told me my dream was right. He did get a backache, and he read *Healing Back Pain* and it went away.

Healing Back Pain is a book by John Sarno that saved my life. My friend Jenine recommended it to me when I was suffering from acute back pain about 20 years ago. Dr. Sarno believes most back pain (and many other symptoms) are caused by oxygen deprivation that occurs when we suppress our emotions.

When Jenine first pointed out the book to me, I was pissed. I thought, "How dare anyone suggest this agony I'm experiencing is all in my head?" Except that wasn't what he was saying. I read the book in one sitting, came up with a kind of mantra/affirmation and said it every time I woke up in pain that night. In the morning, the pain was gone.

It was a miracle. Truly. I've given that book to many people over the years. I guess in my dream I had recommended the book to my boss.

I also dreamed I saw a car go over an embankment and flip over. I ran to the car, but we couldn't get the injured woman out. She curled up into a fetal position. I put my hands just above her and gave her a healing to try to keep her alive until the EMTs arrived. It worked. I saved her life.

The next morning I drove to campus for my permaculture class. Seeing everyone again was like seeing a group of old friends. We did a check-in at the beginning of class. The instructor wanted to know what we had learned this semester.

I said, "I've learned that somewhere along the line, I turned into a control freak. Not about other people, but about myself. I learned that I don't like doing things I'm not good at. I don't want to start things until I know everything. I learned that I can actually do things without knowing everything. I pulled out a whole patch of peas that were infested with aphids. Normally I would have gotten depressed—or at least angst-ridden—about my failure as a gardener. Instead, I figured this was just a learning process for me. Next year I'd do different and better. I've learned that everywhere around me is the potential for abundance. Everywhere around me are solutions. I love that. I've learned to let go."

Yep. I hadn't planned on saying any of that. It just came out, and it was all true. Perfection was not needed—was not even obtainable. I could make mistakes, and it was not the end of the world.

We watched a movie and talked. Then we looked at all our master plans—our poof! plans. We hung the before and after drawings next to one another. It was such fun to see the abundance, the liveliness, the wonderful imaginations of each person expressed in this particular way.

After lunch, we all met at someone's house in Seattle to look at their permaculture garden. Next we were supposed to meet somewhere in Shoreline. I had a map. People offered to take me with them; I should have let them. I ended up driving around for two hours, feeling sick and dizzy in that car, and I never found my class. I did finally find what I thought was the right address, but it looked like a crack house, and there were no cars out front, so I figured it was the wrong place.

It didn't feel like it was the end of the world this time, getting lost. I was not angry at my teacher, my class, or myself. But I was feeling a little sick from the car.

I went back to my place and curled up in my bed. I called my friend and said I wasn't sure if I was up for going out. I'd invited her out to dinner, and now I was canceling. I felt like a wimpy jerk. I told her I'd call later.

I got some food from the refrigerator in the hallway. Then I put *Pride and Prejudice* in my computer, got under the covers, and vegged out. My dizziness and nausea settled down. I called my friend again and we decided to go out.

She picked me up when it was still light, so I suggested we drive to the Medicinal Herb Garden. We had both taken Tom Cowan's Celtic Shamanism Two-Year program, along with his Faery Doctoring workshop, so I knew she would appreciate the garden. We parked and walked along the curving tree-lined street. And then we were in the garden, walking from this garden bed to the next.

It felt like fall had set in: Many of the herbs had no flowers, some of the formerly plump stalks had dried out and turned beige and golden. Of course, this wasn't any different from the evening before when I'd been here, but I noticed a bit more about the garden this night than I had yesterday. The *pièce de résistance* was the ancient cedar tree. My friend noticed that it seemed as though it was really two trees: one tree was enveloping another.

It turned dark quickly, and we were soon driving around Lake Washington down a dark and narrow road. I was so exhausted that my anxiety was vanquished, and I only thought vaguely about the possibility of crashing into oncoming traffic. We passed the Japanese Gardens. Then we were out of the woods and on Madison Avenue. My friend parked the car, and we walked to Cafe Flora.

We had a great dinner and great conversation. I was still a little spacey and dizzy. This often happens to me when I'm one on one with someone. I don't know what it is. Some kind of unconscious stress or shyness emerges—or tries to emerge—but I tamp it down so hard that I don't feel any emotions: I just feel sick.

It ain't easy being green, and it ain't easy trying to figure me out.

Anyway, we had a good time, and then I went home to sleep.

I had nightmares about people trying to kill me. I also dreamed Mario and I saw a jaguar in the woods. The jaguar was walking away, but he turned and saw us. Then he started coming our way. This was quite frightening as we tried to figure out how we'd get away from him.

I got up early, ate, packed, and put everything in my little nauseating rental car. I said good-bye to my little room in the basement; then I left.

It was great getting to school and seeing everyone in my integrative environmental science class. Many of them were in my permaculture class, too, and a few asked me what happened, where had I been yesterday afternoon.

I said, "I drove around nearly two hours trying to find the class. But I couldn't find you all. I guess my role in the forest garden is to get lost."

I laughed and shrugged. It was good to see that my perspective had changed over the last two months. I didn't take it personally that I couldn't find the class; I didn't take it personally that I had gotten lost. It wasn't a character flaw on my part or a rejection by the community on their part.

I just got lost.

Should have gone with someone else.

No big deal.

We started presenting our final projects. Three of us had individual projects. The rest of the class had worked in pairs or in triads. The teacher had posted the order of our presentations: I was last. I wondered if everyone would be exhausted by the time I presented, but I didn't worry about it. If they were tired, I'd change it. I was good at sussing the energy of a group and then flowing with it.

The first presentation was on climate change. Three of the students were working to help the city of Seattle go carbon-neutral. During their presentation they showed NPR's Robert Krulwich's five-part cartoon video called *Global Warming: It's All About Carbon*. (It was so funny. I highly recommend it.)

That was the highlight, but the others were good, too. One duo talked about the green belt in Seattle. Another talked about a transit station going up in their neighborhood. They were all different. All informative. Everyone was engaged and enthusiastic.

And I was last.

Before I started, I had the other students push away the tables and put their chairs in a circle in the middle of the class. I asked them to leave all computers and cellphones behind. Someone asked why, and another student said, "Because she doesn't want us texting during her thing." She smiled. "I don't know what I'm going to do."

She was exactly right. I had noticed people texting and checking their email while others were presenting. I wanted to see what would happen if we were all in a group really together, elbow to elbow, breathing each other's air.

At first, some of the students looked quite uncomfortable. I explained that they were each going to take on the role of someone else, a real person from my community. I wanted them to act and ask questions from the viewpoint of that community person. I would tell them afterward what really happened at the real-life presentation that I had given a month or so earlier.

"You already know everything I'm going to say about a permaculture and ecological garden," I said, "but it was mostly new information for the community when I made the presentation. I also gave you information about these people's personal lives because it's important to realize that everyone working on a project has something else going on in their lives. We've all got people we love who are in trouble. Or we're struggling with our health or our jobs. Something."

I had written up the biography of each person and put it into an envelope and sealed it. On the outside I put the name, sex, and age of the person. Most of the community members were well over 60 years old. I instructed the students not to open the envelope but just to take in the name, age, and sex.

"If you're working in communities and neighborhoods,"

CERTIFIED

I said, "you will often be working with people who are very different from you. I am often the youngest person in the room and that's been true for a long, long time. I think it's good to be aware of the differences and to not judge people just because they're older than you are or because they live in a rural community, or whatever. It doesn't mean they're stupid or uneducated. Some people live away from the city by choice."

I instructed them to open the envelopes. Then I began my presentation: telling the "pretend" library community about the permaculture garden I wanted to put in around the library building. The energy of the group quickly shifted. People were soon asking me questions from the viewpoints of their "characters." It was quite invigorating. One person was concerned that things wouldn't be neat enough in the garden. Another person wanted it to look more wild. Someone else was worried about the cost.

I answered their questions. One person kept asking the same question again and again. I wasn't quite sure how to answer the question differently. But the person asking it was very perceptive: Often in these kinds of situations, people do ask the same question again and again, even after you think you have answered the question adequately.

It was a wild and crazy presentation. Very dynamic. I loved it. I felt like we were a real community. I was laughing when I ended it, and I thanked them all.

We remained in the circle to close. People thanked me for my presentation. We talked about our time together. And then it was time to go.

As usual, I was the first to leave. I got in my little rental car and drove out of Seattle. I remembered how lost and alone I had felt when I first started this program last summer. I had felt so out of place. I was older than almost everyone. I was one of only two people who lived in a rural area. I had felt like a country bumpkin around a bunch of young city people.

But none of that had been true. Or rather, none of that was real. I had been projecting my own fears onto this experience. Once I let go of those projections, once I relaxed a bit and recognized my part in my frustrations, once I gave myself a break, reality was made visible.

The reality was that these were great classes where I had learned a lot about my world and myself.

But something else happened during these ten plus weeks.

I faced some facts about my life—always a difficult thing to do. I had a family member who was struggling with drug addiction. She had gone into rehab for three months, and she now had the skills to help herself and to get help, but she wasn't doing it—at least she wasn't doing it enough to keep herself from relapsing. Every day for weeks, I had worried about getting a phone call from someone telling me she was in a coma or a car accident. Every night I feared I would get a call from someone telling me that she was dead.

I tried to get her help from afar. I tried to talk with her and encourage her. But I was often speaking to her when she was high, and I didn't always know the difference. Later she wouldn't remember what I'd said or anything about our conversation. And she lied so fluently, so easily. Lying is the second language of addicts.

We hear again and again that addiction is a disease. I knew that. But I kept telling the rest of my family, "If it's a disease, then we have to get her help. You don't tell someone who's having a heart attack, 'if you really want help, you call 911.'" How could it be a disease AND one still had to get help themselves?

For a long time, I didn't understand that it was affecting me. Then I realized that my family member's addiction was ruining my life. It was affecting my husband. It was affecting everyone in our family. Different family members had tried to help her. My father, only six months out of dangerous heart surgery, travelled from Michigan to Arizona to stay with her. She remained straight while he was there, but as soon as he was gone, she relapsed. I thought seriously about going to live with her for a time, but then I had a flashback to the last winter when I'd gone to Arizona: I had spent half my time trying to save her.

And I couldn't save her. If I went down to live with her, I would be miserable, and it would just delay the inevitable: She had to save herself. At some point, she had to decide to stop using.

I had started this program in Seattle because I felt hopeless and helpless about the oil gushing into the Gulf of Mexico. I had wanted to save the Gulf of Mexico. I have always wanted to save the world.

I have always wanted to save this particular family member. I felt like I had been trying to save her my entire life.

Once she told me she wanted someone to love her so much that they'd feel like they'd die if she died. She wanted someone to love her so much that they'd give everything up for her.

I told her no one would ever love her like that: no one except herself.

She had to save herself. She had to grow up and save herself.

My relative isn't alone in this desire. I've heard other people say similar things. They're waiting for someone else to save them. Some politician. Some leader. Some spiritual guru.

It ain't gonna happen.

We've got to grow up and save ourselves. It is a profound lack of maturity which causes us to put our heads in the sand.

We've got to act like adults and solve some problems.

My family member is comfortable in her addiction. I think many of us are comfortable in our addictions—we are comfortable with our discomfort.

I know I am.

Or I was.

I now know I can't save my family member. I hope she can save herself. I hope she can love herself enough to put herself first. To save herself.

I was extremely uncomfortable during the course of these classes. I made so many mistakes. I made so many judgments. I was hard on my classmates and teachers. I was very hard on myself. But I kept doing the work. I kept going forward. And eventually, through all the smoke and mirrors I was tossing up, I saw the possibility for abundance. For abundance in the world and in my life.

It won't always be comfortable. It will definitely be messy. But I know we can plant it, grow it, build it, create it, let it happen.

Poof!

There it is.

I got home safe and sound after my class. Fell into the arms of my sweetheart.

Ain't it grand?

Feeding the Dragon, Part 1

October

I decided to take just one class in the fall: The Political Ecology of Food and Consumption. It was a small class, and I'd know half of the people in it. Plus it was on a subject I was fascinated with: food.

Many of my novels revolve around food, one way or another. *Mercy, Unbound* is about a girl who won't eat. In *Coyote Cowgirl,* no one has seen Jeanne eat for twenty years. She ends up as a chef at La Magia Restaurant, creating truth-telling dishes for the little community of Sosegado, Arizona. In *Broken Moon,* Nadira brews chai and tells life-saving stories. In *Church of the Old Mermaids,* part of the novel takes place as the characters eat dinner or breakfast.

You get the idea.

I've had issues with food for as long as I can remember. The last really delicious meal I recall was one I ate right after my grandfather committed suicide. I was eleven. Neighbors and friends brought over food after he died. The Hungarian woman down the road made chicken and dumplings and apple pie and brought them over for us. I remember the chicken melted in my mouth. And the apple pie was so beautiful: The crust was golden and the apples were just sweet enough. The smell of cinnamon filled my nostrils.

A few years earlier, my mother had what they called a nervous breakdown. It was most likely postpartum depression or postpartum psychosis. She had essentially stopped cooking (or doing much of anything) while she tried to deal with her mental illness. My father was working full-time, but he did his best to get all five of us children fed. Essentially, we hadn't gotten a lot of good-tasting meals during those years right after my mother's breakdown.

Then my grandfather died, and I got a good meal. That felt strange. Before I started my first year of high school, I developed an eating disorder. This was in the late sixties, early seventies, before people even knew what an eating disorder was. I was terrified of being fat when I started high school. If I was fat, I believed, no one would ever speak to me. So I watched everything I ate very closely. If I ate too much, I threw up.

By the way, I wasn't fat. I probably weighed about 90 pounds.

Fortunately I only binged and purged for a few months. I started high school and stopped worrying. Well, at least I stopped worrying about whether I was fat or not.

Unfortunately one of my younger sisters emulated my behavior, and she developed a full-blown nearly lifelong eating disorder.

When I was in my early twenties, a doctor told me I was allergic to the world, including most of the food in it. This was a terrible diagnosis for someone like me. I became terrified to eat anything. I'm certain that I didn't get many of the nutrients I needed during this period of time. This no doubt exacerbated my struggles with depression.

CERTIFIED

Today I try to buy only organic and sustainably grown food. I am gluten-free, dairy-free, corn-free, nightshade-free (at least I try), and mostly meat-free. I hope I won't be eating this way forever. And while I long for community, it feels impossible. Most people bond over meals. I usually can't eat anything everyone else is eating, so I don't bond with anyone, and they don't bond with me.

For this Politics of Food and Consumption class, we were going to spend a day eating each other's food as part of our final project. (We each had to prepare a dish that was meaningful to us.) I was fairly certain I wouldn't be able to eat anyone else's food, so I felt a bit of anxiety about this. I contemplated dropping the class, but I finally decided to go for it. Maybe taking this class would heal some of my fears around food.

Before our first residency, I got started on the readings. First up was Brian Wansink's book *Mindless Eating: Why We Eat More Than We Think*. He does research on our eating habits to see what gets people to eat and what doesn't. Restaurants and food companies use this research to help figure out how to lure us into eating more.

Wansink found that most people think they are immune to advertising or to any kind of manipulation. His research has shown that just the opposite is true. How the menu is worded, how the restaurant is lit and decorated, what kind of music is playing, and where the food is from can make a difference in how people feel about the meal they just ate.

For instance, lots of Chinese restaurants have loud music and bright colors. This gets people to eat quicker; this way the restaurant has more turnover. An Italian restaurant is often dark and quiet, with soothing music. People will linger for longer periods of time. That way they eat and drink more, and they're spending more money.

In one study, Wansink and his researchers served everyone

the same wine, for free. For half of the group, the label on the bottle indicated it was from North Dakota. For the rest of the group, the label on the bottle indicated the wine was from California. Guess which group rated their wine superior? Yep, the people who thought they were drinking California wine. In reality, it was the same wine (Wansink, 19-23).

He also found that when people eat with other people they eat more. And the amount each person eats goes up with each additional person in the group. (Although I'm guessing that figure doesn't go up forever.)

People also underestimate how much they eat. Wansink conducted one experiment where they put a hole in the bottom of a bowl and inserted a tube from below so that they could keep filling the bowl with soup as people ate. (The "eaters" couldn't pick up the bowl, and they didn't know about the hose.) The researchers kept track of how much everyone ate. Nearly all eaters thought they ate one bowl of soup when in reality they ate much more.

People who ate from normal bowls (without a hose) ate about 9 ounces. The people who ate from the bowls with a hose were still eating when the researchers stopped them. The "typical" person ate 15 ounces but some ate more than a quart.

Both groups of people estimated they had eaten between 123 and 127 calories. The people with the normal bowls had eaten 155 calories. The people with the hose had eaten on average 268 calories. (47-56).

People were using sight to gauge when to stop eating, not when they were no longer hungry. (Check out his website http://mindlesseating.org/.)

As I read his research, I kept thinking: We don't know when we aren't hungry any more.

At a Super Bowl party, Wansink and friends kept bringing chicken wings to the partygoers. When the researchers would remove the bones from sight and bring more chicken wings, the people kept eating the wings almost nonstop. On the tables where they left the bones, the people didn't eat quite as much (37-39).

What Wansink learned is that Americans seem to keep eating whereas people in other cultures (particularly the French) eat, and then they're done. They don't eat until they're sick or too full. They eat a meal, they enjoy it, and then they go on with their lives.

I don't know many people who enjoy what they eat. They wolf it down and then look for more. Including myself.

Wansink also determined that if people put just 20% less on their plate each meal, they'd lose 25 lbs. in a year (34-35). And they wouldn't even notice it. Most diets don't work because people notice the difference and they feel deprived. Then they fall off the diet and binge.

I also watched a talk by Marion Nestle and read her book *What to Eat*. Both she and Wansink talked about how supermarkets try to get us to buy things that aren't good for us or that we don't need. Supersizing everything makes us think we're getting a deal, but we're just eating more than we should.

They both suggested shopping on the edges of the grocery story. We get into trouble when we go into the aisles: the wilds of an unhealthy food forest. Too many misleading labels. Too much "fake" food. These stores are overwhelming and overstimulating for a reason. Maybe if you get lost or overwhelmed, you just start grabbing at things to buy.

After all my reading, I was excited to go up for my first residency.

Mario planned on coming up with me to Seattle this time. Since I was only taking one class, I thought it would be fun for him to drive up with me. I also thought it would help my stress level. I made reservations at a hotel we'd stayed in before.

They didn't use pesticides, and they hadn't done any recent remodeling. And it was only a couple minutes from campus.

I decided I needed to do something else to help calm me when I went to Seattle. I had four more courses to take over the next year, so I needed to figure out some way to be there and feel relaxed and safe. So I did a meditation—a kind of journey—to the spirit of Seattle. I told Seattle I meant no harm. Asked for permission to come again. Asked if I needed to make an offering. Seattle said it wanted plum sauce. It was a big old dragon-like creature, and it wanted plum sauce.

Yep.

Now you might think this is crazy. Maybe it is. Logically it doesn't make sense. But logic doesn't work for everything. Since I was a kid, I have talked to the land, the trees, the clouds, the animals, the weather. And always, always, always, it makes a difference to my experience when I acknowledge and honor the presence of everyone and everything in a particular space: the Visible and Invisible.

I come in peace, peeps. Wherever you are. And whatever you are.

At the last minute, Mario decided not to come with me. He doesn't like Seattle. My feelings were hurt for a little while. Wouldn't it be worth going to Seattle to spend time with me? But I didn't want to push him.

The traffic to Seattle was fine. I still felt a little dizzy and off-balance after a recent bout with vertigo. I wondered if my days of long drives were coming to an end. I easily found my hotel. Their parking spaces were all sold out for the night, so I had to park in the street. This made me a bit nervous, so I put the Irish *fath fith* on the car to keep it from harm.

I hoped the burglars and vandals understood Celtic charms.

My room had a kitchen so I would be able to cook. I put the food I'd brought with me into the little fridge in the room, and

CERTIFIED

then I went for a walk around the block. It was a hopping Friday afternoon sliding into evening. Across the street from the hotel was a health food store. Nothing much in it for me, but I bought a cashew date bar. Next to the store was a closed used book store. Across from it was an Indian restaurant.

I was buoyed by all the people, stores, restaurants. Being here was going to be so different from being in my basement room in the Quaker House where I was away from everything and everyone.

I felt a little strange. I wondered what all the people around me saw when they looked at me. Did they wonder why this old lady was walking around Seattle alone? Was that how people viewed me now? They saw my white hair and my broken nose and dismissed me as nothing and nobody?

I had someone tell me that once. About fifteen years ago. She said she saw me walking around the neighborhood, and she just figured I was this little shy nobody. And then I opened my mouth and spoke, and she changed her mind about me.

And that had been before my hair turned white.

Since when did I care what the hell anyone else thought?

Oh come on. We all care a little bit.

I didn't like this new mind worm. "You're old, you're old, you're not even bold."

Oh man. Sometimes the mind is . . . a hideous thing.

I went to the all-night grocery. I nodded to the homeless man selling papers. He looked healthy and well-groomed. His eyes were clear; his smile was friendly.

Usually when I go into a grocery store, I get depressed because there is so much I can't eat. This time I looked around the store as though I was researching it.

What were the powers that be for this store trying to get us to buy? What was the narrative of this store? As I came into the door, I saw flowers. Beyond the flowers, in semi-darkness, was case after case of wine. And then the produce.

The Days of Wine and Roses . . . and Vegetables?

I left the store and went back to my hotel room. I called Mario and excitedly told him about the bookstore I knew he'd love, about the all-night grocery store, and the nearby Indian restaurant. He sounded sad and said he wished he had come.

After I got off the phone, I remembered I hadn't gotten the plum sauce yet for the dragon of Seattle. I went back into the night and headed for the all-night grocery store. I passed the homeless man again, and we exchanged "hellos." I told him I'd forgotten something. "Good thing you remembered," he said.

I found a clerk right away and asked where I could find plum sauce. The clerk took me to the plum sauces and asked me what I was going to use it for—so she could help me find the right kind. I couldn't say, "To appease the dragon of Seattle." I mean, I could, but she'd be fitting me for a straitjacket.

So I fibbed. "Spring rolls," I said quickly. Too quickly. Who would use plum sauce for spring rolls? Yuck. I couldn't think of anything else. I should have said moo shu. I kept thinking, "Well, I don't actually eat plum sauce because when you cook plums the oxalic acid becomes inorganic and can be harmful to the body."

But she didn't need to hear about oxalic acid or the dragon of Seattle.

She took me to the plum sauces. They didn't have a lot of plum in them. Corn. Sugar. Would the dragon care?

Or was it the thought that counted?

I bought the plum sauce.

When I came out of the store, the homeless man asked what I'd bought.

"Plum sauce," I said.

"Mmmm," he said. "That sounds good."

CERTIFIED

I couldn't lie to the homeless man. I didn't tell him it was for fake spring rolls. But I didn't tell him about the dragon either.

I said, "Yes, I hope so."

Then I bought his paper.

What a pleasant man he was.

I went back to the hotel. I put stones around the plum jar, to create a little plum sauce sacred area. I laughed. Sometimes it was fun being me.

I turned on a baseball game, muted the sound, then put on a *Deep Space Nine* disk on the computer. Multi-media.

Tried to sleep. The room was too hot.

I managed.

In the morning, it was raining.

I packed and loaded the car. Then I went to the hotel's little courtyard where I was surrounded by plants, and I left the plum sauce behind.

Off I went to class.

We were in a tiny windowless room.

It was awful.

I went inside the room and immediately got dizzy. The fluorescent lights flickered. I was horrified.

How was I going to sit in this tiny room with 16 other people?

I left the room and wandered the building wondering if I should drop the class. I could take something else, maybe one of the required classes from my advisor. Her class was in a big room with lots of windows and lots of space.

I went back down to the car and called Mario. I wept. I tried to ground myself. I was so sick of feeling sick. Why couldn't I walk into a room like any normal person and not notice anything?

I stood outside the car and stared up at the gray sky. I drank the tears from the clouds. It was hardly raining. I used to call this kind of drizzle cloud sweat. Maybe it was dragon sweat.

Maybe it was the dragon letting me know that I could navigate this watery realm.

I went back to class.

We introduced ourselves to one another. The instructor wanted us each to tell a food or farm story. I told both. About my grandfather who owned a farm, who worked it and had another job. He had bad hay fever, and yet he still wanted to be a farmer. Until he took a loaded shotgun, stepped off his land, and shot and killed himself.

Then nothing was ever the same in our family. Ever. The farm I had practically grown up on was gone, over.

Everything changed.

I told them I still remembered what I ate on the day of his funeral: chicken dumplings that melted in my mouth and the best apple pie I had ever had in my life.

We then talked about food in general. Our instructor suggested that changing our eating habits or buying responsibly wasn't enough to change the world. This bothered at least one activist in the room. People want to believe that doing "little" things are revolutionary. My experience has been that we need more. We need policy changes. We need a cosmic shift. A paradigm shift.

The professor also showed an alphabet poster where each letter was the first letter of a particular brand. We went through the entire poster to see if we could name the brands. "K" for Kellogg's. "T" for Tide. Etc.

I was pleased that I didn't know most of them: I had not been branded. I was disturbed that most of the other students did know the brands, particularly the younger students. It seemed like it should be the other way around. Did this mean younger people had been exposed to more branding than those of us over forty?

At lunch, I went to talk to my advisor who was also the director of our department at that time. I mentioned how hot and cramped we were in the classroom. She explained they didn't have enough big rooms for everyone, so the classes with more students got the bigger spaces. Although I understood the logic of what she was saying, it still felt like poor planning on their part. I thought about dropping the class, but I liked the professor and the subject.

My advisor wanted to know how I was doing, and I told her I felt quite isolated. Seattle was a tough town to navigate, and the students I encountered weren't very friendly. I said that hardly anyone talked to me. She said, "Did you ever consider that they might be intimidated by you?"

I said, "No." Why would they be intimidated by me?

She suggested that my experiences in the world might leave some of them tongue-tied. I doubted that, but I didn't argue with her. I had to get going.

The instructor had told us to go to Whole Foods for lunch: We had to walk through the entire store and then pick a section and figure out the narrative of the store.

I walked to Whole Foods and then wandered through the entire store. I'd been there before. It was huge. I felt a bit dazed, as I often did in these big stores. In the produce department, I stood and looked at rows and rows of beautiful, colorful fruits and vegetables. Two young nice-looking men were putting the produce out. They were friendly and answered my questions. As I looked at this beautiful food, I wondered how any of us ever ate anything else.

Then I sat in some nearby chairs and watched people. One man by himself at the bulk bins looked quite befuddled. He started to take filberts and then changed his mind and was going to get cashews and then changed his mind again. He finally got almonds. I noticed quite a few confused-looking people.

What was the store's narrative? As far as I could figure, they were saying, "Come to this beautiful, peaceful place where we have all the answers. Whatever you buy here is healthy, and you'll live forever."

After lunch, the class discussed our experiences at the store. And we talked about the readings.

Then it was over. I felt invigorated by the experience, despite the awful room. How we get food and who gets food is a social justice issue. What you eat or *if* you eat determines how healthy you are—or if you'll live at all.

Change the food we eat, and the world changes.

One in seven people in the United States lives in poverty. Over 20% of the children in the United States live in poverty. In all likelihood, this means they are subsisting on junk food because junk food is cheaper for people who don't have the time, knowledge, space, or financial resources to cook.

We produce enough food in the world so that no one needs to go hungry. And yet hunger still exists.

It was a good class, and I had much to think about.

But I was ready to leave the dragon of Seattle and head home.

Feeding the Dragon, Part 2

November

During the month between residencies, I read *The End of Overeating* by David A. Kessler. Dr. Kessler, the former FDA commissioner who worked to expose the tobacco industry, wrote this book to try to figure out why he and other people overeat.

I wanted to know the answers to this, too. I've had issues with food all of my life, including bouts of anorexia/bulimia before I started high school and then bouts of cravings for sugar and carbs the rest of my life. The cravings always felt beyond something emotional: They felt physical.

Kessler discovered many things, but what fascinated me the most was what happened to rats when they were fed a junk food diet: They ate until they were obese. And when Froot Loops were put out in an open field—where rats normally don't go because that's where predators can find them—they raced out into the open to get their Froot Loops, apparently not caring about the danger (Kessler, 33).

Scientists discovered that a combination of salt, fat, and sugar causes pleasure neurons in our brains to fire, and the more we eat foodstuffs in this combination, the more neurons fire. When Kessler talked to researcher Sara Ward at the University of South Carolina at Chapel Hill, he asked her about the combination of fat and sugar being a "stronger reinforcer." How strong was it, he wanted to know. She said "the breaking point at which . . . animals will no longer work for the reward . . . is slightly lower than the breaking point for cocaine. Animals are willing to work almost as hard to get either one" (31).

Wow. Doesn't that put a different spin on the idea of using willpower to stop overeating?

Kessler also learned from one of his sources, a food executive, that the food industry understands the tendency for particular food combinations to create cravings and the desire to eat more and more: They design food to have layers of fat and sugar and salt to stimulate these cravings (18). They also design foods that people don't have to chew: a kind of "adult baby food." People will eat this food quickly and eat a lot of it before their stomachs have time to signal that they were full (95).

When I read this, I remembered Marion Nestle had said she didn't think the food executives were sitting around a table trying to figure out how to make people fat, diabetic, with heart disease. They were trying to figure out ways to sell their products. I don't think tobacco executives sat around a table trying to figure out how to give people lung cancer and emphysema either. They were trying to figure out ways to sell their products to people. It was the same thing, it seemed to me. Was there any difference between the part of the food industry that was trying to sell addictive and unhealthy products and the tobacco industry trying to sell addictive and unhealthy products?

After I read Kessler's book, I lost a sugar and carb craving I had had for several weeks. It felt like a bucket of cold water had been thrown over me, and it reset my brain. At least temporarily.

CERTIFIED

For the class, we had two projects to do over the month. One was to go to a grocery store we didn't normally frequent and try to figure out the narrative of the store. Mario and I went to a Safeway in Lake Oswego, which is an upscale town close to Portland, Oregon.

The building looked half a century old. Inside, the lights were low, the music on the sound system was mellow. I didn't see any children and only one man. Mostly middle-aged women (and older) walked slowly around the store shopping. Huge signs over the produce declared: Organic, organic, organic! Then all through the store were these yellow cards touting the discounted price if you had a "club card." I figured the narrative of this store was you can be mellow and classy (because it was a rich town) while being smart and saving lots of money.

The second project in my food class was a "commodity challenge." We had to abstain from eating anything with corn or soy in it for 48-72 hours. I thought this would be easy breezy since I was so accustomed to depriving myself of different food stuffs. And I didn't eat corn, anyway, or much packaged foods.

It was not breezy. We also could not eat animals who had consumed corn or soy. This meant no eggs. Then I discovered packaged gluten-free rice tortilla had xanthan gum in it. I knew this was a kind of bacteria fermentation. What I didn't know was that it was often cultivated on corn or soy. So that was out. I learned that ascorbic acid (which is in my organic fruit spread) was also probably made from corn (along with citric acid). That was annoying. But since I couldn't have my rice tortillas, I didn't have anything to put jam on anyway.

All those years I thought I was corn-free, I wasn't.

Very annoying.

I was able to eat well easy enough: rice, beans, vegetables, salmon. But I did get cranky having to watch everything I ate even more carefully than I normally did. Plus I felt tired most of the day since I didn't get much protein in the morning. (Legumes may be protein, but I don't get the same kind of clarity and energy I get when I eat animal protein. I wish it weren't true, but it seems to be. I was vegetarian and vegan for many years. It didn't work for me.)

I stopped my soy and corn fast at 42 hours. Then I went out and got an Amy's gluten-free pizza.

One Tuesday, Mario and I decided to drive to Seattle to hear Marion Nestle speak at the University of Washington.

Yes, I agreed to another four-plus hour ride to Seattle when it wasn't required for my classes. We left a couple hours early, so I could show Mario around the city. I journeyed to the Dragon of Seattle ahead of time. This time the Dragon wanted me to bring a dragon to the Troll. (Yes, I know how this sounds. But I just see it as bringing a gift for your host when you go to their house for dinner.) So I brought a small red Chinese dragon with me.

The drive to Seattle was much easier and more fun with Mario along. We got lost trying to find Cafe Flora, but we pulled over and looked at the map together and figured it out. Mario used to have a lousy sense of direction, and I had a great one. When we moved to the West, everything switched around: Now he knows how to get everywhere. And I don't.

We had a great late lunch/early dinner at Cafe Flora, and then I drove Mario to see the Troll. We couldn't find it at first, but I kept driving around, since everything looked familiar, and finally we were driving up Troll Drive and there was the Fremont Troll. I left the red dragon in the Troll's hand. Then I took Mario to the Medicinal Herb Garden on the campus of the University of Washington.

After all that, we went to Marion Nestle's lecture on the U of W campus. She covered much of the same ground as she did in her books and on the video I had seen. She talked about how the food industry was now targeting children with their marketing.

CERTIFIED

And the food industry balked at every attempt to get truthful and complete labeling.

She often acknowledges how difficult reading food labels is. When she shops, she first reads the labels on packaged or frozen foods. If the ingredient list is long and incomprehensible, she puts the package back. If the ingredients are food ingredients, then she checks the serving size. (I got these gluten-free English muffins once and looked at the label and calories, sodium, etc. The calories and sodium seemed a bit high, but I thought it would be all right every once in a while. I forgot to check the serving size, which was A HALF a muffin. They're still sitting in my freezer uneaten.)

Next, if the calories seemed low, she looked at the per serving for calories, fats and sodium. "If these are big fractions of the Daily Values," Marion Nestle writes in *What To Eat*, "I leave the packages where they are . . . I watch the sugars. To keep my intake of sugars below 10 percent of my daily 2,000 calories, I can only eat the equivalent of four tablespoons (60 grams) a day" (Nestle, 304).

Still a wee bit confusing.

I'm not sure it was worth the time and money to drive to Seattle for this particular lecture, but I was glad to see and hear Nestle in person.

Mario and I got safely home.

When it was time for the second residency, Mario agreed to go to Seattle with me on Friday. We got caught in heavy rush hour traffic, so it was after dark when we got to town. We were hungry. Before we checked into our hotel, we met my Seattle friend at Cafe Flora. I had the Autumn Root Roast: celery puree with chanterelle mushrooms, parsnip and butternut squash hash and wilted beet tops. The dish was a bit too salty, but beyond that, it was scrumptious. And the conversation was great.

Afterward Mario and I checked into our hotel, the same one I had been in last time. It was late, so I couldn't take Mario around the neighborhood. We turned out the lights, got into bed, and Mario fell asleep almost immediately.

I lay in the dark, wide awake, listening to the Friday night revelers outside as they crowed, laughed, and talked.

I turned on the TV once or twice, to see if it would lull me to sleep, but it didn't have a timer, so that didn't work. I couldn't turn on the light because that would wake Mario. I hadn't brought my computer because I wanted to travel light.

I didn't sleep and I didn't sleep and I didn't sleep.

Crap.

I couldn't believe it. I had brought Mario to make everything better. Easier.

And I couldn't sleep.

I finally fell asleep around 3 or 4:00 a.m. I was awake by 7:00 a.m.

Fuzzy, cranky, and wobbly as hell.

Mario drove me to school. I had talked him into going back to the hotel and hanging out, maybe doing some writing. He had wanted to check out when I left for school. Something about him going back to this old hotel and being in our room on the second floor, overlooking part of the city, seemed calming to me. And romantic. As though he was going to a hotel room in Paris.

At school, our class was in a different room from last time. It was bigger and had windows, and we switched off the fluorescent lights. I was so happy with this turn of events.

In the morning, we talked about our experiences with the commodity challenge. At least half of the people had done the challenge wrong. They had continued to eat dairy, eggs, and meat. The instructions seemed very clear in the syllabus. No one had an explanation about why they had done it incorrectly.

Then our instructor asked us to describe a favorite Halloween candy and what it meant to us. (Since it was the week after

Halloween.) As we went around the room, I was astonished at the stories about all these different candies. And not a one of them seemed embarrassed to talk about how much they loved candy.

I thought, "But isn't candy for children?"

I could not remember the last time I had bought candy, except for Halloween to give out to the trick or treaters.

I wondered if this was an age thing. When I grew up, eating candy was a treat. We didn't have candy in the house, except after Halloween. When I was in junior high, I would sometimes walk down to the drug store after school and buy a Three Musketeers bar. Or when I was a young kid, I would run down to the five and dime if we were in town on a Saturday. I'd stare at the bins of candy for a long while until finally I'd pick up and buy a hard candy we called a jawbreaker.

That was about it.

It felt strange listening to people talk so fondly about candy. It seemed too personal. Shouldn't people be ashamed of such things?

Of course not.

Yet, it still felt weird.

I told the class I didn't eat candy. (I must have sounded like such a prig.) But I did remember enjoying candy corn when I was a kid.

I told them I liked Halloween because it was my mother's favorite holiday. It was the only one she seemed to really participate in. Dad took us out trick or treating and then when we came home, Mom had decorated the kitchen table and put out apples and cider and caramel for us. She seemed happy and involved with our family.

That's why I liked Halloween. Not because of the candy.

Anyway, we had other discussions. At lunch, I found Mario

sitting downstairs, so we went to a Vietnamese restaurant that had one gluten-free vegan dish. A bowl of vegetables and noodles.

In the afternoon, our class listened to several speakers. One was a woman who worked for the food industry. She did research to find out how, what, and where people ate to help the food industry market to people. I kept wondering if she did the kind of research that enabled food companies to design addictive food we didn't need to chew.

She was currently doing research on Americans eating alone. Unlike most people in other cultures, a lot of Americans eat alone. She said we in the U.S. eat 45% of meals alone. 20% of people eat meals in a car. Americans eat more separate meals. In a family, the husband might eat something different for dinner from the wife, and the children might eat something different from either of their parents.

We also heard from two women from Nicaragua and one woman from the Philippines. The woman from the Philippines talked about how things had changed now that they were mining the mountain near her. She said, "I exist because others exist." They had been healthy and strong because they understood the connection with the mountain. They buried their ancestors on that mountain, only they didn't call it that: They planted their ancestors. Now the water and air were polluted.

The Nicaraguan women talked about fair trade. How fair was fair trade? The prices were often too low still for the workers and farmers to make a living even when it was called "fair trade."

Even though this was all interesting, I could barely stay awake. My three or four hours of sleep were not enough. The class ran long, but I was anxious to get out of town before a storm was set to hit. We had planned on leaving at the end of class, 4:30. I hated driving in the dark and the rain. I asked the instructor if I could go, and then I left.

Mario and I got to the car just as it began raining. I had

CERTIFIED

wanted to stay overnight so we weren't driving in the rain, but Mario wanted to leave right away. I felt like I had dragged him to Seattle on his days off, so I agreed to leave on Saturday after class even though I thought it was dangerous.

We weren't on the expressway ten minutes before I regretted that decision. A torrential downpour began. Soon passing cars in six lanes of traffic were spraying water everywhere. Our tires seemed to barely touch the pavement. I had my hands up in front of my face several times, waiting for a crash. I was so stressed I could barely contain myself. I wondered if I was going to have a stroke or a heart attack.

I got angry. I yelled at Mario for not wanting to stay in Seattle. He glanced at me dumbfounded. I kicked the inside of the car. I growled and cursed.

I was so sick and tired of being scared to death all the time.

I told Mario I didn't actually blame him. I blamed myself for not doing what I thought was safe. For not doing what I knew would feel safer for me.

We kept driving until we got to the food co-op in Olympia. We stopped there to eat and for me to calm down. I wanted to stay until the rain stopped. (In April?)

At the co-op I got rice cakes and macaroon chocolate chip cookies. (So much for not eating junk as a response to some emotional crisis.)

We sat in the car and ate rice, sweet potatoes, salmon, and vegetables. And then I began eating the cookies.

I started to calm down.

As though I had taken a tranquilizer.

We got back on the road. It was raining less.

Or else I couldn't tell the difference.

After I ate three cookies, I realized they didn't taste that good.

I ate the rest anyway.

We arrived home safe and sound around 9:30 p.m.

I decided I couldn't do this anymore. I was going to quit school.

I emailed my advisor that I was done after this class.

Thanks for the memories, but I was outta here.

Let Them Eat Cake

December

I felt relieved when I quit school.

Life could go back to where it had been before I started in June.

No one would miss me.

Yep, I was relieved.

I didn't like quitting something midstream, but I had always said it would be all right to quit if school wasn't working out. Besides, I was more interested in the sustainable food certificate, and that was impossible because one of the required classes was only offered in the winter, and I couldn't take it because I would be in Arizona for the first residency.

My advisor answered me the next day. She said I'd have to fill out a form. She didn't say she was sorry to see me go. Nothing. Just that one line.

I had wanted to go to this particular school because I didn't think I'd only be a cog in a wheel. I thought they would be flexible and change their requirements to meet my needs. I wanted to fashion a certificate around what I was interested in, what would most benefit me.

That wasn't quite what they had in mind. And I understood that from a bureaucratic point of view.

Still, I wanted to do things my way.

A couple hours after I'd received the email from my advisor, the teacher for my Political Ecology of Food and Consumption class wrote to me and said he wanted to figure out a way I could take his food systems class in the winter.

Wow!

Just like that, things changed.

I wrote back, yes, yes, yes!

Suddenly everything was different. Now I could change to the Sustainable Food and Permaculture certificate. I wouldn't have to take at least two classes that I was dreading. I looked up the requirements for the certificate. I could do an independent studies for part of my electives.

I loved independent studies. I thrived when I could work at my own pace and do my own thing.

I emailed my advisor and told her what had happened and that I was changing to the sustainable food certificate. And I said I wanted to take an independent studies.

She wrote back that the department didn't allow independent studies any more because it was contrary to their goal of helping students to learn to collaborate.

Then why the heck did they advertise it as part of their program?

I was quite annoyed.

I called her and insisted I wanted to take an independent studies. She told me they had something they called special topics. Students did their own projects, but then they came together once a month, on the Monday of the residency weekend, to discuss their projects. I told her it wasn't viable for me to stay in Seattle for two extra days to sit in a room for three hours to talk about my project.

Perhaps I could work it out with the instructor, she suggested.

I asked her what she thought of my plan to change certificates and do one class as an independent study. She didn't think it was a good idea, but it was my certificate. I could do whatever I wanted.

It wasn't the food certificate she objected to; it was the independent studies.

I told her I'd think about it, and I got off the phone.

I found out the instructor for the special topics was my food class professor. He was already letting me miss the first residency because I was going to be in Arizona in January. I didn't like asking for too many favors.

But I asked. I told him about the independent studies I wanted to do, and I said I couldn't be at the Monday meetings. He said we'd work something out.

I did wonder if it was smarter to stick with the ecological planning and design certificate. Would it be easier to find a job with that under my belt? Who was going to hire someone with a sustainable food systems and permaculture design certificate?

It didn't matter. I was much more interested in the classes I had to take for the sustainable food systems certificate. I wanted to write about food. I was interested in sustainable food, and I had been since I was a girl.

My husband laughed at the whole process. He thought I was always "working the system." Gaming the system, finagling my way into and out of things. He wasn't being judgmental: He admired it. I said I was just trying to get the most out of the experience. I didn't want to sit through classes that didn't interest me, especially given how much the classes cost.

I filled out the form and changed my certificate to Sustainable Food Systems and Permaculture.

With that decision made, I concentrated on my final project for my food class. For our last residency, we needed to make and bring a dish to class that had meaning for us. We also had to make a video and be prepared to talk about our dish during the residency.

I had lots of ideas. Most of them involved soups. I loved making soups. My mom used to make the most amazing soups. Mine were never as good as hers, but I liked making them because they are very forgiving. You can leave ingredients out or add new ones. Plus soups are hard to burn. I was notorious for starting to cook something in the kitchen and then leaving the room and forgetting all about whatever I was cooking. (Been doing that all my adult life, so it's not an age thing.) I have ruined an entire set of Creuset pots (and now they're so expensive we can't afford to replace them). And more besides them.

Whatever I made, I had to get this dish up to Seattle. Soups would not be easy to transport. I decided the easiest thing would be to bake something, like a carrot cake. Carrot cake had meaning to me because Mario and I had a carrot cake as our wedding cake. It was a sheet cake made by a local baker in Ann Arbor who used whole wheat flour and no sugar. It was our announcement to the world that our life together would be wild and whacky.

Carrot cakes also had meaning to me because my friend Michelle and I had created a recipe for a carrot cake that was gluten-free, dairy-free, and sugar-free, and it was delicious. I loved being able to make a cake that I could eat and other people enjoyed, too.

I was so excited about the prospect of making and talking about this carrot cake that I decided I was going to write a book about it: *The Carrot Cake*. I started doing research on each and every ingredient in the cake. I spent days talking to growers and produce managers and producers. I loathed talking on the phone, but that was what I did. I learned more about carrots than I would have ever imagined. And I wrote it all down.

I was fascinated by all of it.

I intended to finish the book by the last residency, but I soon realized that it would be more fun to have time to breathe. I decided I would finish the book over the next six months.

I then made my video about the carrot cake, incorporating a lot of what I had learned doing research for the book. I used my computer as the video camera. I did some test pieces. They were difficult for me to watch. Ever since my nose was broken and distorted by nasal polyps, it's been difficult for me to see myself in the mirror or on camera. I can almost forget about that sorry and sad part of my life, until I see it in the flesh. Until I see me in the flesh. I felt ugly and not like myself when I saw how I looked.

But we all change, if we are lucky. Life is played out on our faces. My life had not been easy, and it showed. So what?

I did the video.

Now I had to figure out what my final presentation would be. I could talk all about carrots, like I had on the video. I could talk about why carrot cake had meaning to me.

At first I wanted to make a video I could present to the class. My classmates could watch it, and I could hide in the background and not have to talk to anyone. I could stand far enough from the camera that they wouldn't notice my distorted nose. (Yes, it is funny the illogic we come up with.) I figured this would be easier on them, too, since they must all see me as loathsome as I saw myself. I wasn't one of them. I was so much older, so much more battered.

Oh man. What kind of tape was playing in my head?

Where had all this insecurity come from? Life was more fun when I was arrogant and sure of myself. Too many years of illness had left me . . . not full of myself. Because of illness I had had to quit a full-time job. Since then, nothing had seemed exactly right. I had been used to having a place in the community. I had been used to having a "regular" job.

Now I struggled to make a living through my writing and a part-time library job I did from home.

As I was going through these various humiliating thought processes, it occurred to me that I needed to stop trying to be someone I wasn't. I didn't want to be a business executive or even a director of a non-profit. I didn't want the hustle and bustle of a forty-hour a week job where I was in charge of everything. Maybe I had at one time.

I was a storyteller. I forged connection through stories. I foraged in this world and that world and then brought everything together and created a story. Baked a story? Cooked a story?

Still, I told Mario, "They're all really into videos and texting. They seem very comfortable staring at a screen and getting information that way."

"Probably most of them have never heard a story live," Mario said. "With a real person telling it."

OK. That possibility sold it. I was going to tell a story about "The Carrot Cake That Saved the World, Or At Least Part of It."

Soon it was time to make the carrot cake. I set aside an entire day to do it. I had all my ingredients in the house, including lots of carrots.

Before I started, I drummed a bit. I sang to the directions and to all the plants that were going into this carrot cake. I had dreamed years ago that I was in the kitchen with an older Romanian woman, and she told me, "You must always talk to the spirits in everything," including food. So I do. I asked the Invisibles to make this a healing and nourishing cake for all.

Then I started the creation. I ground cinnamon, allspice, and nutmeg into powder from their whole forms. I milled quinoa for the flour. I mixed these dry ingredients together with some baking soda and powdered ginger.

I grated two cups of carrots. Then it was time to make the carrot juice. I cut up some carrots and started feeding them into the juicer. Suddenly the juicer started "walking" and then vibrating so fast it looked like it was going to fly across the room. I tried to hold it down, but it was too powerful for me. It started spinning—like that girl in *The Exorcist*—while spewing out orange vomit. I was terrified this thing was going to fly across the room and kill me. I pulled the plug, then ran from the room.

Eventually the juicer stopped spinning. I had quite a mess to clean up, but nothing was broken and no one was hurt. I called the Champion Juicer company and asked what had happened. He was pretty sure I needed a new blade. I said, "Whether I need a new blade or not, it doesn't seem like it should do that. I could have been seriously hurt."

He seemed unperturbed by this possibility.

Juicing carrots was out, but I still needed carrot juice. Fortunately Mario was in Vancouver. He stopped at Whole Foods on his way home and found organic carrot juice in a glass jar.

Once I got the juice, I continued to make the carrot cake.

Tragedy averted.

Here's the recipe:

Kim and Michelle's Cosmic Carrot Cake

Dry ingredients:
- 1/2 cup arrowroot
- 2 3/4 cups quinoa/millet flour mixture, freshly milled

1 T baking soda
1 T fresh cinnamon
1/4 tsp sea salt
1/2 tsp fresh allspice
1 tsp powdered ginger
1/4 tsp grated nutmeg
2 cups shredded or grated carrots

Wet ingredients:
1/2 cup agave syrup
1 3/4 cups fresh carrot juice
1/2 cup water
3/8 cup olive oil
zest of one lemon
2 T lemon (a little more won't hurt)
2-3 inches ginger, grated
1 tsp vanilla extract
1 egg (whisked)

1. Mix the dry ingredients together EXCEPT FOR THE CARROTS. Mix well.
2. Mix the wet ingredients in a separate bowl. Mix well.
3. Add the wet to the dry. Then add the carrots. Pour the mix into a glass lasagne dish.
4. Bake at 350° for 60 minutes or until knife comes out dry. (I think I baked mine 40-50 minutes.)
5. Let cool and add your favorite frosting. I used the one from Blossoming Lotus's *Vegan World Fusion Cookbook*.

CERTIFIED

Mario and I left for Seattle Friday afternoon. It was already dark out, but it wasn't raining or snowing, so I was grateful. The ride up was peaceful and uneventful. We drove through downtown Seattle at night. All the buildings were lit up. A huge star hung over Macy's. It was beautiful.

We found a place to park right in front of the hotel. After we checked in, we walked around the neighborhood. Then we went to bed.

Mario fell right to sleep.

I did not.

I tried watching *Pride and Prejudice* on my computer. That did not put me to sleep. I watched TV for a bit. I tossed and turned.

I got out of bed and read an issue of *Shambhala Sun*.

I went back to bed.

I finally fell asleep around 4:00 a.m.

I woke up around 7:30 a.m.

Mario made me oatmeal for breakfast. I put together a lunch in case there wasn't anything for me to eat at the Interpretive Feast. Then I went out into the cold morning and drove to our instructor's house.

I got lost once, but it wasn't a big deal. With a little help from Mario on the other end of the phone, I got on the right track again.

My teacher greeted me at the door. He showed me where the kitchen was, and I put away the carrot cake and my lunch. Most of my classmates were already gathered in the living room. I went and stood near them. When I said I was feeling wobbly from lack of sleep, two of the women offered me their seat. I said no at first, but then I sat with them.

"As long as you're not giving me your seat because I'm old . . . er."

They laughed.

Soon the house was full, and it was time to begin our presentations. Because I had brought desert, I was scheduled to go last. I wasn't happy about that. By late afternoon, I might forget the story I was going to tell. But I decided to just go with it and not worry about it.

The first presentation was about pancakes. We watched a video, and then my classmate made pancakes on a hot griddle in front of the class while she talked about what pancakes meant to her. She did a great job, and soon everyone (except me) was eating pancakes.

Next up a man talked about enchiladas and what they meant to him and his family. After his video played, he made eggs on the griddle while he talked. I scooped up some enchiladas (on the side of the casserole so that I wouldn't get any cheese). Then he put an egg on top of it for me.

It was delicious. Spicy and chewy.

And so the day began.

I can't remember all of the dishes. Some I could eat, some I couldn't. There was cabbage soup, some pastries, a dip, an Israeli dish with tomatoes and eggs, ravioli, smoked salmon, grits. I ate the tomatoes and eggs, the grits. I even had some organic hard cider.

I liked the hard cider. Besides a sip of beer a couple years ago and a sip of wine 15 years before that, I hadn't had anything to drink in decades. The hard cider didn't make me sick or dizzy. It didn't make me high. It just tasted good.

I loved the personal stories that came with each dish. I liked that the professor's seven-year-old son was a part of the day. I loved that we talked about these dishes in the context of our lives and our cultures. At one point I looked around at everyone as a woman discussed her dish, and I thought how lucky I was to be a part of this event. I didn't want to be anywhere else in the world. I was actually a part of it, instead of feeling apart from it and everyone else.

In the middle of the day, I noticed I had a voicemail. I went outside and listened to the message. A Family Member said one of my sisters was in trouble. The Family Member sounded like she had been crying or like she was stoned. My heart raced as I called her to see what was going on. It seemed like something happened to my family every time I went to one of these residencies. The Family Member was incoherent: It was obvious she had been using drugs. When I told her she was incoherent, she said she was just waking up from a nap. I remembered when my youngest sister was still drinking, she had often used a similar excuse when I asked her if she was drunk: "No, I'm just tired," she'd say.

Oh, so that's why you're slurring your words?

I ascertained that my younger sister was not in any danger. My sister and the Family Member had just had an argument. So I hung up the phone and went back to the feast.

Fortunately, I was able to forget about my family and enjoy the day. This was new, too. Perhaps I was actually learning some new skills: How to live life and not worry by just not worrying. Why hadn't that ever worked before?

It didn't matter. I was enjoying myself.

At the end of the day, it was my turn. Everyone was ready to go home by now, I was certain.

But I was going to tell them a story anyway.

I sat in a chair at the front of the room, and I told them about a woman named Grace who could have lived in a village or a city anywhere in the world three days ago, three weeks ago, 30 years ago, or 300 hundred years ago. Her community was dying. The land was infertile. There were no jobs, and the people were sick. Grace didn't know what to do. She went to the Old Woman who lived at the edge of town, in that betwixt and between place, because Old Women always know the answers to everything.

Grace asked the woman how to save her community. The Old Woman said, "That's simple. Make them a cake. It must contain these ingredients: You must find that which holds all life. You must find an edible stone that carries the souls of the ancestors. You must include the god-given Mother grain brought to the people by the dove. You must find the spice that the goddess Chango built her lunar palace from. You must find that which feeds the dead and makes them immortal. You must find the spice that will give you visions or make you mad. Find the plant that is the goddess Mayahuel. Find the oil that anoints the dead and kings alike. Find the tree that originated in heaven and is sacred to all, with its feet in water and head in the fires of heaven. Find the tree which gives all that is necessary for living and that came into existence after it sprouted from the head of the first person to die. Find the ashes of the phoenix because in those ashes are the spices you'll need. And most of all, you must find the honey underground, that food which does not get its sweetness from the heavens, the bees, or the birds."

And so Grace went around the world for three days, three weeks, 30 days, or 300 hundred years. She found what she needed: an egg (holds all life), salt (an edible stone), quinoa (god-given mother grain), cinnamon (what the lunar palace is made from), ginger (put in the mouths of the dead to chew), nutmeg (visions or madness), agave (goddess Mayahuel), olive oil (anoints the dead and kings), dates (originated in heaven), coconut (provides all that is necessary for living), and allspice (from the ashes of the phoenix).

She brought all these ingredients back to her village. But she couldn't make the cake because she hadn't figured out what the honey underground was. She went out and stood in her overgrown and neglected garden and looked around. She didn't know what she could do now to save her people. Then she heard a whisper, or maybe it was just the wind, but she looked down and saw some frothy greens growing from the ground. She reached down and pulled on these greens and up came this golden orange carrot: what the Celts called the "honey underground."

She thanked her garden for this unexpected gift. Then she made her humble carrot cake. And once she fed it to the villagers, her community and the people in it began to thrive and all was well again.

Grace didn't write down the recipe, though, so people all over the world have been trying to duplicate it ever since. I told the class that I thought I may have finally figured out the recipe, and I made this carrot cake with that recipe. This cake would surely heal and nourish them all.

As I told this story, no one moved. A couple people closed their eyes and listened. They seemed mesmerized. When I was done, someone said, "What a perfect way to end the day."

I enjoyed myself thoroughly. I felt full of myself again, in that glorious way when you know you are yourself.

I cut up the carrot cake and passed it around.

I noticed a couple people didn't finish their tiny piece of cake. It was a little chewier than normal, a little denser than it usually was. I wasn't sure why, but I tried not to fixate on it. The story was good, and most people ate the cake.

Our teacher talked for a bit, and then it was time to leave.

I felt like I had been a part of and a witness to an extraordinary event.

I followed a car belonging to one of my classmates out to the expressway, so I wouldn't get lost. Then I drove back toward the hotel. I was soon mired in a traffic jam.

Ah, Seattle.

Eventually I was able to get away from the jam. I parked

outside the hotel. Just then I got a call from my sister. She told me about the fight with the Family Member. She decided she needed to go to an al-anon meeting.

Our whole family probably needed that. It was difficult having an addict as a family member. It was difficult to keep from being angry with that person for throwing away her life.

Later I talked to the Family Member on the phone. She still sounded stoned to me, and usually I won't talk to her when she's like that. But I did. She essentially said it was her choice to deal with her life this way. And I agreed it was.

Even though I wanted to shake her and tell her to knock it off.

I wondered if she would end up living in the street or dead from an overdose.

It was so terrifying and frustrating.

Mario and I went out to eat. Then we came back to the hotel and sat on the bed eating the rest of the carrot cake while we talked.

That night after Mario went to sleep, I lay next to him with my hand on his neck. I could feel his pulse under my fingers. I thought about the day, about the food and the stories, about my man curled up beside me.

I felt so grateful for my life and for this day.

I closed my eyes and fell asleep.

In the morning, we went to Cafe Flora for breakfast. Then we went to Elliot Bay Books, down the road from Cafe Flora. I bought Dale Pendell's *Pharmako* trilogy. Mario bought lots of books. Then we drove to the Medicinal Herb Garden.

Most of the herbs had been cut down for the winter. Some beds had nitrogen-fixing ground cover. Some of the herb beds were filled with dried leaves. The black cohosh still called to me, even though it had almost melted into the soil. And the hawthorn tree. Tiny red berries hung from the thorny branches. Figs hung from the fig tree, looking like tiny shriveled purses.

Mario told me that when I walked amongst these plants, I looked most like myself.

I was so glad to have him with me this time.

Soon enough we returned to the car and headed home.

Getting Out

January

For the first month of the winter quarter, I was in Tucson, Arizona, where Mario and I lived for six weeks out of the year. We typically each wrote a book there, and I visited family and did research on border and/or conservation issues in the Southwest. For my Special Topics project (my independent studies), I wanted to research the life and death of a jaguar who had lived in the wilds of southern Arizona, in the borderlands, for sixteen years, more or less.

The first few weeks in Tucson were difficult. I had a sinus infection that tired me out; plus my asthma was acting up. It was unseasonably cold in Tucson, so it was difficult to be outside (because the cold triggered my asthma). I was also trying to get the reading done for my Food Systems class and arrange for interviews for my Special Topics project.

On top of that, I was driving to and from Scottsdale about once a week so that I could be with my family. I was exhausting myself, and I wasn't getting enough rest. I was torn: I wanted to be with my dad, and I wanted to get as much research done on the jaguar as I could.

My father had had heart surgery a year before where he had been dead on the operating table for five minutes. Fortunately, they were able to revive him, and a year later, he was doing well. He seemed in good spirits. My brother-in-law who had had the stroke also seemed to be doing well, although he still had some trouble with one leg and one arm, and pain medication kept him sleepy much of the time.

I didn't talk with my Family Member who was abusing prescription drugs. As far as I could tell, she wasn't using while I was around, but I didn't engage her in any personal dialogues. She had told me it was her business if she wanted to use drugs, and I accepted that. I could see she was struggling with her life, and I wished I could help, but I didn't know what to do. Addiction is such a solitary disease.

In Tucson, I began interviewing for my jaguar project. I first talked with a biologist who was passionate and still angry about the death of the jaguar. The jaguar had been "accidentally" snared and then collared. About two weeks later, the taggers noticed the jaguar wasn't moving. The animal was airlifted out and taken to the Phoenix Zoo where the vets there said he was in kidney failure. They subsequently put him down. After that, the proverbial shit hit the fan: Who was to blame for this terrible loss? I was trying to sort out everything that happened by talking with as many people involved as I could.

One day, Mario and I drove down to Douglas, Arizona, which is on the U.S./Mexico border. We followed a washboarded road out to a cattle ranch. Although the ranch was only sixteen miles from town, it took us an hour and a half to get to it because the road was so bad. We later learned that the road used to be a fine dirt road, but the increase in the border patrols had caused the ruts. The ranchers could no longer get suppliers to come out to the ranches because of the road.

For several hours, I talked with the ranchers about the jaguar and jaguar conservation. They fed us lunch and answered all my questions. They were hospitable and frank, I believed. And they were frustrated by the change in the quality of their lives because of what was happening at the border. Things had shifted in the last few years, they said. As security got tighter around the cities, the border traffic had to go somewhere: People were now crossing the border in the desert and travelling across their ranches.

The amount of trash left behind by these travelers was astonishing. The ranchers talked about being up in the mountains in places where no one hardly ever went and they would find diapers and other garbage left in formerly pristine water holes.

The kinds of people crossing were different now than they had been in years past, too, according to the ranchers. They believed the drug cartels now ran all the operations, even the people-smuggling operations. The ranchers used to help anyone in need on their property, but since one of the ranchers was murdered last winter, they were hesitant to get near anyone who was crossing their property. Instead, they called Border Patrol. Although they were grateful for the stepped up security, the traffic had ruined their road. And the amount of money spent was exorbitant, with little effect. They thought worker permits should be issued for the migrant workers, just as they used to be. At least one rancher believed that marijuana should be legalized. Marijuana was the primary drug being smuggled out in their region.

I asked if all the border traffic affected the wild life. It affected their cattle, they said, so they were fairly certain it affected the wild life, too. Many wild animals were nocturnal and came out to hunt and feed at night. That was also when many people illegally crossed the border.

CERTIFIED

Mario and I headed home around dusk, driving down the pitted dirt road through some of the most desolate country I had ever been in. It was slow going, and I wondered what would happen if our car broke down. During the day when we had come out to the ranch, we had seen one border patrol truck after another, racing up and down the road, throwing up dirt and dust. Now we saw no one.

At one point, I spotted a small whirlwind of dust, pink from sunset, rise up from the road ahead of us. I stopped the car to observe it and try to figure out where it had come from. As I looked more closely, I realized it had come from a huge hole in the road about the size of our car. I had stopped the car just a few feet from disaster. Our car would not have made it out of that hole unscathed.

I drove around the hole and continued even more slowly. Fortunately we made it off the road and onto pavement safely. The ranchers told me that they often got cracks in their windshields and had to get windshields fixed and axles replaced. They had tried to convince Homeland Security to pay for a new road since the Border Patrol vehicles had caused the damage. Homeland Security said it was the county's problem. The county didn't have any money. So it went around and around. In the meantime, the ranchers had to live with the road as it continued to deteriorate.

I was glad I didn't have to travel it often.

Some days later, I interviewed a couple of hunters and conservationists. They were still hurt and angry about the death of the jaguar, and about what had happened afterwards: the blame game. They felt they had been treated unfairly by the press. I also talked with two people from a government agency, and they also believed they had been pilloried by the press.

I began reading transcripts from the investigation of the

death of the jaguar. I read press accounts. I read books about ranching and wild life conservation.

I believed everyone I had talked with were good and decent people. And yet a magnificent animal had died. One man had pleaded guilty to violating the Endangered Species Act when he admitted he had tried to snare the jaguar. Another woman was awaiting trial on the same charge.

I knew I could write about this subject, and I could write about people pointing fingers at one another. That book would probably sell. But what good would it do? If some of the players were already distrustful of one another, how would that help? I didn't want to write anything that would disrupt jaguar conservation in the United States any more than it already was.

In many ways, it seemed extraordinary that this jaguar had made his living in Arizona for sixteen years. It could be argued that everyone I spoke to helped keep the jaguar alive during that time.

My feelings and beliefs about conservation and environmental work were evolving. And they had changed dramatically in the years since I left Michigan and moved out West. When I lived in Michigan, I had believed that if the government owned the land everyone benefited. My childhood had been spent in the fastest growing county in the United States. I saw farmlands and woodlands turned into subdivisions. We had to drive up north to see one old growth tree. I grew up hearing one environmental horror story after another. Someone had to do a better job than what regular people were doing: Why not the government?

In the West, I saw government agencies buying up land, but they often didn't have the funds to care for the land properly. Where I lived, blackberries would take over land that had once been worked by humans and was now owned by the government. Inevitably, they'd hire someone to come out and spray pesticides

CERTIFIED

on the blackberries. How was that better than having a farmer or someone else own the land and care for it themselves?

I had seen land ruined by cattle. I had seen land ruined by farmers. I knew it could happen, but it didn't have to. If the landowners (or leasers) followed sensible conservation practices and didn't overgraze or over-plant, land could be preserved—and people could stay on the land.

More and more it seemed to me real changed happened when everyone put down their bundles of rhetoric, came to the table, and figured out solutions.

Of course this didn't always work. I had been in many meetings with people who could not and would not see other points of view.

Yet I didn't see any benefit from us all shouting at each other.

In the middle of my research and interviewing, Gabrielle Giffords, Tucson's representative in Congress, was shot in the head at a Safeway store in Tucson where she had gone to meet with her constituents. Although the man who shot her and killed five people was mentally unstable, many of us wondered if the intensity of the political debates—especially in Arizona about border issues—had somehow exacerbated his mental illness. If you constantly shout, "shoot the gun, shoot the gun, shoot the gun," eventually someone is going to shoot the gun.

We have too much violence in our culture. And vilifying someone who doesn't agree with us has become standard operating procedure, and I believe it's a form of violence. I wanted to make certain that I didn't vilify anyone when I wrote about what happened to the jaguar. I just wanted to find the truth.

I also went to Mexico to visit a rancher who had taken all the cattle from his ranch and who was now restoring the land

and doing what he could to encourage wild life to live on the land. After I spent the day with him, I wrote an essay about the experience called "The Wild Keeper" which became part of my book *Under the Tucson Moon,* and I've also made it available for readers of this book in the appendix.

To Home

February

I was only back home from Arizona for three days before Mario and I packed up the car and headed for Seattle.

The next morning I attended my Food Systems and Their Alternatives class for the first time. (I had missed the first residency since I was in Arizona, but the professor had sent me a recording of the class.) Most of the other students had been in my other classes, and it felt good to not be such a stranger in a strange land this time. I remembered how isolated I had felt a mere six months ago, how no one had talked to me, how I had felt like a pariah.

Originally I had wanted to do this particular program so that I could feel like I was a part of something. When I'd first gotten here, I had felt more isolated than ever. Now people actually spoke to me, and I spoke to them. I felt affection for most of them. I thought, "Yes, Kim, you're developing a relationship of sorts with them. That takes time, which was not my preferred way. I'm from the Midwest. I made friends and enemies quickly and easily.

Two of the people in the class were new to me. I introduced myself. I remembered how unfriended I had felt when I first started in July, so I wanted to be as welcoming as possible to any newbies.

We had a check-in at the beginning of the class. Our teacher asked us what we had learned since we started this class or the one last semester. When it came time for me to talk, I told everyone that I was learning to relax. I was learning to go with the flow.

I told them about being at my dad's house. He had made soup and asked if we wanted any. I asked him what kind it was, and I heard him say it was vegetable. I said, "Sure." When he handed me a bowl, I looked at it and said, "Dad, there are chunks of meat in this." "Yes," he said, "I said it was vegetable and beef soup." I shrugged and said, "Take out the meat and I'll eat it."

I hadn't had any beef in over fifteen years. But my dad had made the soup, and I didn't see the harm.

For me, that was an amazing leap.

I also told the class that more and more I didn't see things as us vs. them. Most people were just trying to do the best they could, trying to feed their families and get through the day. My self-righteousness was definitely mellowing.

Then we talked about food systems.

We're trying to look at our food systems and find points for change: leverage points. Is alternative really alternative? If everyone can't afford to shop at a farmer's market, for instance, is that alternative? Have we analyzed the class system while looking at food systems? How does class impact the food system?

People are skeptical about the food system now, but that's a recent trend. We talked about the gap between production and consumption. How is something produced and then what makes someone buy it? That gap is important to understand consumption, our teacher told us. We need to ask questions. There are a lot more organic foods now. But has that shifted any eating patterns? Has that shifted who has access to good food?

That gap—between production and consumption—is where we can make change. Perhaps that is where we can build community.

We had discussed the new normal in our other food class, and I thought about it now as we talked. What is the new normal for people? Is the new normal polluted skies, pesticides in our food, food that isn't food?

We talked about hunger. 45% of those using the food bank in Seattle had secondary degrees. 9% were homeless. 21% owned their own homes. At food banks all around the country, volunteers were the main staff. At first blush, this seems great. But that means if those volunteers go away, so does the food bank. When there is no long-term funding, these organizations are always in peril.

More and more, private companies and volunteers are taking over what was once part of the public domain, part of what the government did. I believed this was because of our country's seemingly unstoppable march toward neoliberalism (deregulation, open markets, capitalism is king, privatization). The markets expand and public programs shrink. The civil society safety net is disappearing. How do we challenge this?

Did Marx say this or someone in class: Hunger is not a problem of agriculture; it's a political problem.

We also talked about our hunger challenge. We were supposed to eat on $7 a day for three days. $7 is what people on assistance in the state of Washington get for food stamps. I had been in Arizona at the time, and it took me five days to finally be able to eat on only $7 a day. It was hard. I didn't like it. I didn't like having to constantly deprive myself.

I had been on food stamps once when I was in my twenties,

living in Bandon, Oregon, after I'd been fired from a job. I think it was only for a month, but I felt humiliated. I had felt like a complete and utter failure. How could someone as brilliant as I believed I was end up like that?

It had been a lesson in humility. Trying to eat on $7 a day when I was on vacation had not been my idea of a good time either.

But eventually I had succeeded.

In the afternoon, we listened to a panel of experts who worked in various parts of the food system. Their resumes were long and impressive. As they talked, though, I learned they made very little money and worked very long hours. I wondered again how this helped promote any kind of long lasting change? If people were constantly willing to sacrifice their wellbeing to work at these service organizations, how would these organizations ever be funded enough to fully reflect the staffing and work that needed to be done to run them?

In other words, what they were doing didn't seem sustainable to me. It may be holy and noble to volunteer or work for very little pay, but that wasn't good for the organization or the long term viability of it. How many wonderful community events or institutions faltered and disappeared once a long time volunteer or underpaid staff person left?

If we are going to make change in the world, we should value our time and talent and get paid adequately, and we need to make clear our needs for real adequate funding.

Mario and I went to lunch and dinner at Cafe Flora. It was great, as usual. We stayed overnight in Seattle. In the morning, we went to Cafe Flora again. By then, I had had enough of Cafe Flora, or any restaurant. I was ready to be home.

My Wound is Food

March

I spent much of the month between the second and third residency doing research for my Food Systems and Their Alternatives class. We were supposed to research the food supply chain of a commodity. I picked agave at first and then decided to research the use of agave in tequila and other mezcals.

As far as I could determine, tequila was not a sustainable product. In the wild, the agave plant was quite hardy. After years of monoculture farming, however, blue agave was now more susceptible to disease and pests. Many growers used lots of fertilizers and pesticides. This exacerbated erosion in the area, and the run-off made its way into the water systems.

Even if the grower farmed organically, the processing for tequila used a great deal of water. Distillers often discharged the hot water into streams, and the leftover acidic agave pulp made its way into landfills. Mexican laws against these practices were generally not enforced. Recently, an American environmental company had been awarded a contract to build a plant in Jalisco to help alleviate some of these problems.

This is a tiny portion of a huge picture about global trade, sustainable livelihood for growers and farm workers, and environmental and business sustainability. The more research I did on the subject the more I wondered if it was possible to maintain sustainability if the demand for a product or service was either high or extremely low. Something in the middle might be just right: the Goldilocks approach to sustainability.

For me, the most interesting part of my research of agave and tequila was the myth and goddess associated with it.

Tequila and other mezcals had their beginnings in the Meso-American drink *aquamiel*, which was essentially the juice made from the agave plant. When this "honey water"—considered a gift from the gods—was allowed to ferment, it become *pulque*, a slightly intoxicating drink used ritually and for the elderly and others in need.

The goddess Mayahuel (often syncretized with the Virgin of Guadalupe in later years) was called the goddess of pulque. She was also a goddess of creation and fertility and is often called the goddess of tequila. In Ana G. Valenzuela-Zapata and Gary Nabhan's book *Tequila: A Natural and Cultural History,* they write that mezcal was truly a blending of worlds, a kind of child of the Meso-American goddess Mayahuel (who brought pulque to the mix) and Dionysus (who brought the ecstasy of intoxicating drinks to the mix). Mezcal (and therefore tequila since it, too, is a mezcal) was a true blending of cultures.

In the early 1600s, the first tequila factory began production. In the late 1800s, the first tequila barrels were exported to the United States. The agave hearts were roasted in earth pits, and as the popularity of tequila grew, more and more trees were cut to feed these pits. Soon the area around Jalisco was deforested. This made it easier to grow more agave. The big producers encouraged the farmers to grow blue agave instead of food crops (Valenzuela-Zapata, Nabhan xxiv).

CERTIFIED

It was also around this time that a plague devastated the agave crop. It turned out the "culprit" was the "worm at the bottom of the bottle. It was a larva that burrowed into the heart of the plant, moving along (destroying agave tissues) until it had ravished its host" (xxv).

Many plagues have followed. Currently agave is being destroyed before it reaches maturity by something the locals call "agave AIDS" (xxv).

During this month of research on agave, I also finished the novel I had almost completed in Tucson, *The Desert Siren*. I continued research on my jaguar project and did my library work—which was the one thing I got paid to do. I had no time for our new publishing venture, Green Snake Publishing, or for any social life. The weather was also monstrous. We had snow and rain and more snow. A friend and former coworker died rather unexpectedly, and we were unable to attend her memorial because of the weather. It was so cold that every time I went outside, I had an asthma attack.

It had been a stressful and busy year.

I had had this fantasy that if I went back to school, I would get well: healthy. I would be normal again. I would be able to work as hard as everyone else. I could be brilliant again, with something to say.

Illness had knocked me off my feet and then took nearly everything else from me: self-esteem, my career, financial stability, a place in the world. I kept trying to get up and start again. Get up and start again.

Get up and start again.

And nearly always, I would start to feel better again, I would work too hard, and I would fall to the ground again.

Breathe deep the gathering humus.

Was going back to school just one more event in a long line of events in my life where I tried and failed to be the person I once was, or thought I once was? Capable, healthy, a valuable asset to the planet.

Valuable *asset* to the planet.

Yuck. That made me sound like an item on a financial report.

The original meaning of the word "value" was to "satisfy a debt."

It meant "enough" to satisfy the debt.

Enough, already.

It is enough. Why did I want to be considered "valuable" by the culture? By society? So I could survive, thrive, be a part of the pack?

It is enough.

I am enough?

I used to be confident, pretty, capable. An *asset*.

There we go again.

School was not making me any healthier.

But I wasn't going to quit now.

It was time for the last residency of this semester. Mario came with me to Seattle. We left our town while it was still light. It rained, but the traffic wasn't bad. Since travelling back and forth to Seattle—or maybe because of it—I had developed a new anxiety: I didn't like driving in the rain.

This was not a good development for a Pacific Northwesterner.

My nervous system just didn't seem suited for modern life any more. Or something. This reality sometimes made me feel weak and neurotic, even though I knew I wasn't weak. I appeared to be wired differently from a lot of other people. I overloaded easily. (Think of me like a house. Inside and outside of this house, a lot of stuff is going on. So my breakers are constantly being tripped. Then they have to be reset again.)

In any case, Mario and I stayed in the right hand lane, didn't go much over 65 mph, and made our way toward Seattle. We got caught in one traffic jam near the Air Force base for an hour and a half.

Eventually we got to Seattle. We stayed in the same hotel we'd stayed in before. Didn't sleep well, but morning came soon enough. Mario dropped me off at my teacher's house, and our day began.

We had five presentations of various food commodities: gelatin, agave, oysters, seaweed, and hops. Everyone brought food to share. We spent the day talking, eating, presenting. I learned that gelatin was in just about everything: including sugar and white wine. This made me angry. I didn't eat pigs and cows on purpose. (Freaking mad cow disease, for one.) But I had most likely consumed it inadvertently over the years. I might rarely use sugar and never drink white wine, but I do eat fruit. Gelatin is one of the ingredients on the stickers they put on fruit. Companies should not be able to put ANYTHING on or in a food product without labeling it.

I learned the reason some male beer drinkers have "man boobs" may be because of phytoestrogens in hops.

I learned oysters in the Pacific Northwest are sustainably grown and harvested, for the most part.

I hadn't been able to master how to make an iMovie, so I used Prezi as I talked about the use of agave in tequila and mezcal. After my talk, we taste-tested tequila and two Del Maguey mezcals that I had brought.

Then it was on to the next presentation.

I enjoyed being with these people, talking about the food system, trying to figure out ways that the food system could be more sustainable. When I first started back to school I had felt so alienated. Now I felt like I was one of them.

As the day went on, I noticed something peculiar. When someone came up to talk with me, I would answer their question and then walk away. What the heck was that? Had I always done this? I was always craving conversation and community, but when I got it, I walked away?

I enjoyed speaking to large groups of people. But one on one, I often wasn't comfortable. I had come into this world shy and I still was, although no one who knew me believed this. I wondered if I had always done this: walked away when someone was trying to have a conversation with me.

Wow. How disengaging was that?

I would have to work on that little quirk.

After the discussion of hops, there was a taste test. Since beer is not gluten-free, I wasn't going to try any. I went into the kitchen and did the dishes while the group taste-tested. I could hear them in the other room laughing and talking. I felt disengaged from it all but not completely separate. It was meditative doing the dishes while listening to all the commotion coming from another part of the room.

The day was over too quickly. We said our goodbyes. I gave out copies of *Coyote Cowgirl*. Mario came in and helped me take stuff out to the car. Then we left.

After I rested at the hotel, we had dinner, wandered around Whole Foods, and then brought chocolate Coconut Bliss back to the hotel and ate it.

When it was time to sleep, I couldn't.

I didn't feel well. I had twitches. And I couldn't sleep.

I tossed and turned and wondered why the hell I had eaten chocolate before going to bed. I kept doing stuff like this over and over.

I was exhausted. I had hardly slept all week.

I finally got out of bed, fumbled around for my computer, and went into the bathroom and closed the door so I wouldn't wake up Mario. I put towels on the floor and then sat on the towels with my computer. I began to write my final paper for my Food Systems and Their Alternatives class. It's called a "learning reflection." I was supposed to look at what I thought I knew about food systems at the beginning of the course and what I thought I knew now.

At the beginning of the semester, I wrote, in part: "The more I learn, the less I know. I used to be certain if people had the facts they would change. I've realized that most of the time that does not work. Our food system feeds a great deal of the population, yet one in four children is food insecure in this country. If we could figure out how to change that reality—so that everyone had good, clean, fair food—then it seems we would have a key to changing our food systems."

As I sat there on the bathroom floor feeling miserable, I started thinking about my grandfather, my father's father, who had killed himself when I was a girl. His suicide haunted our family. It was one of many suicides on both sides of my family.

I suddenly remembered there had been a suicide in the movie *The Truth About Farmer John,* one of the films we had watched for this class. Farmer John's uncle, who had worked the farm with Farmer John's father, had killed himself.

I googled "farmer suicides." I was shocked. Farmer suicides were quite common worldwide. Many farmers were in dire financial straits. It would make sense that they were in trouble emotionally, too, although I had never thought about it.

They were doing a job the world didn't seem to respect or value financially. Small farmers who were connected to the cycles of nature, to their craft, were the ones least respected and least rewarded.

I began writing my paper:

"My favorite first line of any book is in Pat Conroy's *Prince of Tides:* 'My wound is geography. It is also my anchor, my port of call.' The first time I read this book, I wept at the opening line. He articulated so well what I had felt since I was eleven and my grandfather, who was a farmer, stepped off his land, went across the road, and ended his life with a shotgun. The land that had been my anchor, my port of call, was now my wound, and the wound of my family. This farm down the road from our house which brought so much sustenance to others could not heal my grandfather.

"My grandfather was one of many farmer suicides over the years. Although he killed himself in the sixties, suicide rates for farmers is (and has been for some time) higher than the general population. Suicide rates for male farmers in the Midwest are twice that of the general population. In England, one farmer a week commits suicide. In India, between 1997 and 2005, a farmer committed suicide every 32 minutes.

"When I read these statistics, I was astonished. I hadn't ever thought about my grandfather's suicide in terms of anything beyond a family tragedy. Yet now I wondered if Pat Conroy's line could be rewritten to articulate the plight of all farmers: 'Our wound is geography. It is also our anchor, our port of call.'

"The high suicide rate for farmers seemed to say something about the problems of our planetary food system, too."

And then I wrote several more pages. I finished with this,

"In the beginning of this course, I said the more I learned the less I knew. Now the more I learn, the more I realize I've been on the right track all these years. Place, stories, connection, community: These have all been my life's work. I have so often felt like a stranger in a strange land. I couldn't understand why other people didn't hear the varying dialects of each stream and river. Why didn't others wave to the crows who called out each time someone passed by them? Why couldn't others see the 'value' in a tree just because it was a tree? Nobody else I knew whispered sweet nothings to passing clouds. I started to feel like I was a crazy woman.

"But I wasn't.

"I was right.

"We need to be connected to our place and to our food. We need to resacralize our world, but not in a religious sense. The word sacred means 'holy,' and holy means to be 'whole.'

"It needs to be acceptable to talk about place and food and community as something meaningful. As something that makes us holy: i.e., whole.

"It has to be acceptable to discuss the importance of a meaningful life in relationship to our food, work, and food policies.

"Perhaps when we understand that our world is sacred, we will know that the work farmers, growers, and farm workers do is holy: Their work makes us hale, holy, whole.

"Maybe then no farmer will end his or her life in a barn or a cornfield—or across a dirt road in the garage of an old mission house, like my grandfather did.

"Then geography (and food) will no longer be anyone's wound. It will be our anchor and our port of call."

I closed my computer. It was about 4:30 a.m. I crawled back into bed and finally fell asleep.

I awoke three hours later. Mario made breakfast. I was in a daze. We stopped at the Medicinal Herb Garden on the way out of town.

Most of the garden was still in winter mode. But I was drawn to spots of color here and there. Near the fig tree was a nearly black maroon-colored flower dropping toward its dark shiny green leaves. It was called Lenten Rose, Helleborus orientalis. I knew nothing about it. The small green serrated leaves of monkshood/wolfbane had pushed up through the winter detritus.

I pressed my face against the huge cedar tree that always made me think of Yggdrasil. And then I walked to the far end of the garden where I hadn't been before. A few wrinkled dark green leaves of the motherwort had drawn me over to it. Mario and I stood near each other and looked down at the plant. I knew that motherwort was considered a "woman's herb." Lionhearted. It was good for the heart. Whenever I saw motherwort in the woods, I always felt strengthened, as though I could carry on.

Now I stood next to this plant and hoped she would imbue me with some of her strength. I looked around at the dozens of raised beds. I couldn't see all of the two and half acres that made up the garden, but I could feel the liveliness of it all.

Mario and I continued walking. We looked at the identifying cards above each patch of earth. Plants from all over the world grew in these beds. When the garden was in full-bloom, I told Mario, it felt a little bit like being in that bar in the first Star Wars movie, where beings from all over the galaxy had come for a drink and a good time.

Oh, the information these plants must share with each other through their roots, their pollen, through the air. I loved being in their company, even when all I could see was the bones left after the plants had fallen to the ground when they died or went into dormancy.

Come spring, most would rise again.

Mario and I left Seattle. It felt like a long drive home. I was exhausted. I felt somewhat defeated by my self. By patterns I seemed powerless to change. By an illness I seemed powerless to change.

Yet I carried with me the lovely day spent with my classmates. I carried with me the thesis of the paper I had written on the bathroom floor. I am right. Community, connection, crows, trees, clouds: They're all sacred, they all matter.

I carried with me the lion-hearted motherwort.

When I got home, I looked up the plants I had seen at the Medicinal Herb Garden. Motherwort also helped with anxiety.

CERTIFIED

Hellebore was a witch's herb that helped with invisibility, among other things. Only the most adept witch, medicine person, or poisoner could use it in healing. And wolfsbane—aconite—was also a witch's herb. It was a poison used to kill wolves—and maybe werewolves. Painted on a witch's broom, it helped them fly through the night unobserved. (My guess is that it was used to help the shamans—the medicine women—"fly" shamanically.)

All three of these plants had alkaloids, hellebore and wolfsbane at more poisonous concentrations than motherwort. I wondered why I had been drawn to these three plants. Two of the plants were used to help with invisibility. I didn't want to be invisible. At least, not generally. I did want to be lionhearted.

My friend Linda had known the names of most every plant. I have never been good at taxonomy or with scientific names. You call something a particular name, then you stop seeing it as the individual being it is: You just see it as a chair, a window, an oak tree, a boy, a girl. But for healing purposes, it is good to know which plant is which. Before Linda died, she said I needed to be the plant person once she was gone.

She gave me her copy of *The Secret Life of Plants* just before she died. She made me promise to read it. I haven't yet. I heard so many unflattering stories about Peter Tompkins that I wasn't sure anything he wrote could have any truth to it. (Sometimes I am very black and white in my thinking.)

I have always been a tree person. A plant person. I didn't know the names, necessarily. I just knew the plant. Their personalities. I did name the trees in the woods around my house when I was a girl. It wasn't oak tree, or pine tree. They had names like the Lullaby Tree, the Witch's Tree, the Mother Tree.

Plants have helped, soothed, sheltered, and fed me all my life.

I have dreamed of them.

Plants come from the Earth. Are they messengers from the Earth?

Does it really matter what they are and aren't?

They *are* amazing.

I started out last summer being amazed by plants once again during my permaculture class. I have kept coming back to them again and again during these past nine months.

I have kept coming back to them again and again over the course of my life.

I just went to my closet and pulled out the copy of *The Secret Life of Plants* that Linda gave me. I opened it and saw her handwriting inside. She underlined her favorite quotes. She wrote notes in the margins. She left several pages of handwritten notes about the book inside the back cover. She wrote, quoting Tompkins quoting Gustav Fechner, "It is a dark and cold world we sit in if we will not open the inward eyes of the spirit to the inward flame of nature."

And George Washington Carver said, "I learn what I know by watching and loving everything."

What a great way of being in the world.

I think it's time I read Linda's copy of *The Secret Life of Plants*.

Geography might be my wound. Food might be my wound. But plants are my anchor, my port of call, to paraphrase Pat Conroy once again.

Perhaps I can learn from them by watching and loving everything along the way.

Audacious

April

Soon enough it was time for the first residency for my final class: Theories and Practices of Socio-Environmental Change. I wasn't exactly chomping at the bit for this course, but I was actually glad to get away to Seattle. It had been raining in the Columbia River Gorge almost every day since we returned from Tucson in early February. Then Mario had gotten sick, and not long after, I was ill, too.

I was hoping a change of scenery would do us both good, and the class was an excuse to go to Seattle.

It didn't rain for our trip to Seattle, and we encountered no crazy drivers. We drove into town around 9:30 p.m. The city was dark and lit up all at the same time: Some floors of the skyscrapers were black; on other floors fluorescent lights created an eerie glow.

As we drove by the tall downtown buildings, I wondered how many fish were dying in some dam to light this city. The salmon were already on their last legs (metaphorically speaking, of course), in large part due to the dams that cut through our rivers in the Pacific Northwest.

Ah well, nothing I could do about dams this night.

We found our way to our little hotel and went right to sleep. I had asked for a larger room this time, and my request got us a room with two twin beds instead of one queen. The room wasn't any bigger, as far as I could tell. At first I was grumpy about Mario and me having to sleep apart, but then I realized that I might be able to sleep better if I didn't have to worry about waking Mario with my tossing and turning. And that was exactly what happened. I got the best sleep I'd had on any of my trips to Seattle.

The next morning, Mario dropped me off at school. I had no expectations for this class. It was taught by the same teacher as the permaculture class, and we had not exactly connected. Still, I went to the first class with no expectations. I had already read through one of the assigned texts, *How to Re-imagine the World: a pocket guide for practical visionaries* by Anthony Weston, and I loved it. His first sentence reads, "This book is a guide to creative thinking in service of radical social transformation" (Weston, 1).

Before he begins his first chapter, he writes, "Radical imagination begins with a move beyond compliance and resistance, beyond reactive tinkering or hunkering down or cynical accommodation. The first big move is to an alternative picture of how things could be instead (7)." Yes, yes, and yes. He writes about vision. For me this was so important. I sometimes got lost and dragged down by all that I knew: or thought I knew. By all the impossibilities. So I was ready for some visionary thinking in this class—although I was not expecting it.

I probably knew about half of the students in this class of twelve. Two of the other students I had had in nearly all of my classes, and I gave them each a big hug. It was nice to see two friendly faces, and I was happy they were in class with me.

After we all checked in, we watched part of a video about the artist Andy Goldsworthy. Mario told me later we had seen the film, but I didn't remember it. This time I was entranced. We watched him try to build a huge cone (or egg) out of stone at the beach. He got partway done four different times and each time the stones collapsed.

He decided he didn't understand the stone enough. He needed to learn more. Instead of doing the same thing over and over, with the same results, he listened to feedback from his environment. For some reason, this reminded me of all the politicians who seem so proud of never changing their minds and always sticking to their dogma as though that was something to be proud of. Instead, wasn't that a little insane? Goldsworthy observed and listened to feedback, and he changed what he was doing. Ultimately he created his new cone.

The tide came in and covered the cone. Goldsworthy said he was giving it to the sea as a gift and he knew the sea would make more of it than he could ever hope for.

It was fascinating watching his process. He was incorporating some of the principles of permaculture we had learned: to observe and interact; to catch and store energy. And he had a vision that he didn't try to control.

Afterward, we broke into groups and discussed the film, from a permaculture viewpoint.

Then it was lunch. Mario picked me up, and we went back to the hotel. I ate the lunch Mario had prepared for me. It felt cozy being in this little hotel room that was more like an apartment with its tiny kitchen and tiny living room. For some strange reason, I felt like I was in Paris again. Maybe because we were on the second floor, and we could hear and see a bit of the city.

The rest of the class was walking to downtown Seattle for our field trip that afternoon. Since I was just getting over the flu, and I was still trying to hack up a lung every few minutes, I decided I wasn't going to walk on such a cold day. After lunch, Mario dropped me off at Pioneer Square near the Percola, where we had all agreed to meet.

I stood in the cold and in the welcome sunlight and waited for the class. How interesting that once again I was alone and separated from the class. Briefly, I wondered if it would turn out like the time we went to the Medicinal Herb Garden when I had ended up in the wrong place and waited for everyone else for about an hour. More or less. I had felt stupid and alone.

Today I felt none of those things. I knew if I somehow missed the class, I could just keep walking to the building where we were going to be for the last part of the afternoon.

I watched several tour groups gather at various spots around the square. This was the place where the underground tours began and ended. I pulled my scarf up closer to my mouth and huddled down into my jacket as I listened to the indistinguishable murmuring all around me. I felt strangely comfortable standing in the middle of this bustling city.

I was no longer a stranger in a strange land.

At least not completely.

At the International Sustainability Institute, Todd Vogel talked to us about greening Seattle's alleyways. Alleys were always intended to be a vital part of the cityscape, yet so many of them were now used only for service vehicles, criminal activities, and as dumping grounds for garbage and drug paraphernalia.

ISI cleaned up their own alley and collaborated in creating a city wide "green alley" design contest. During the World Cup, they showed the games in the alley and got huge crowds.

CERTIFIED

I enjoyed the tour of the green alley immensely. It looked like any other alleyway, only it was clean, and no windows or doors were boarded up. A wrought iron table and chairs were situated near one door. A hanging garden was *in medias res* (the metal container had just recently been added to the side of the building).

After we looked over the green alley, we all headed back toward school. I only got about half way. I was having trouble breathing, so I called Mario, and he came and drove me the rest of the way.

For most of the afternoon, we discussed the big project for this class. We were supposed to "identify and design a collaborative connection involving two organizations which, to your knowledge and/or intuition, do not interact, collaborate or consider one another as allied resources toward social and environmental change."

I had been thinking about this project for over a month, since I had first heard about it, and I hadn't come up with anything. I kept thinking of connections that had already been made: having the hops from the brew pub be used as compost for a mushroom grower, using grease from restaurants for biofuel. Things like that. I knew so many of the players in my little part of the world, and I knew (or thought I knew) that they would never collaborate or help one another.

My brain hurt from trying to figure it out.

The teacher told us that this project should be fun. If it wasn't fun, we were doing it wrong. He encouraged us to be audacious. Come up with an audacious idea where two entities would cooperate for the benefit of all.

I loved the idea of being audacious.

I loved that word.

I had to be visionary.

I always said I was a visionary.

I had to be audacious.

I had to have fun.

I was on board with all of that.

By the end of the day, I was flagging and didn't feel well. I was glad when it was time to quit for the day. Apparently I wasn't completely over the flu. Mario and I had planned on having dinner with a friend, but we weren't able to get a hold of her so we decided to skip it. Besides, I wasn't feeling well.

Mario got takeout from an Indian restaurant next door instead. It was not very good. We ate it all.

By the end of the evening, Mario had developed a cough, usually a sign that he was coming down with something.

The next morning, it was cold and rainy. We didn't go anywhere to eat. We didn't even stop at the Medicinal Herb Garden. We left town about 8:00 a.m. and headed south.

On the four hour drive home, I kept trying to think of a project. I couldn't. Every idea I came up with provoked only exhaustion. That was how I can usually tell something is not for me. If I had a novel idea and then I got tired, that was a clue that I shouldn't write the book.

Our teacher had suggested that we think about our project as though we were designing a job for ourselves. I tried to think about what kind of job I wanted.

I didn't want a job. I wanted to write.

Beyond that: What?

I didn't want to manage a library or an organization any more. I wondered out loud if that was a sign of depression. I didn't get excited about working for an organization and making change on a local level. Why not? Was I giving up?

I was interested in writing.

But I had gone back to school so that I could get a job. Had

CERTIFIED

I spent all this money and gone through all this stress to decide I didn't want a job?

No. I had always known I didn't want a job job. I wanted to make my living by writing.

But absent that: What?

Maybe it wasn't depression. Maybe I wasn't giving up. Maybe I had just changed. I couldn't get excited about running a business or a nonprofit. I no longer looked at famous activists and thought of myself as a failure because I wasn't one. I didn't want fame and never had, but I did want to be useful. I didn't want to be a speaker on a circuit. I didn't want to be a teacher.

Yes, those were all the things I didn't want to be.

What did I want to do?

I wanted to tell stories.

I wanted to write.

I loved writing novels. That was my passion. I enjoyed nonfiction, too, although it was much more difficult for me. When I was working on the carrot cake book, I enjoyed the research. It was an amazing amount of work, doing the research, tracking down leads, getting people to talk to me. It was especially difficult for me because I didn't like talking on the phone. Still, I enjoyed the research. I was good at it. Putting it all together into a book was more difficult.

Recently the local food network had sent me their research on food security in our area, and they told me they were always looking for researchers and writers. (My heart had done a little leap when I read that. I was excited by the prospect of delving into all that data. Page after page after page of useful stats.)

I thought of myself as a wild child, out wandering the forest or getting down and dirty in my community making change. Yet in true life, I didn't actually enjoy community building processes. I wanted to. I wanted to be a part of a vibrant community. But I wasn't particularly good at building relationships—or I wasn't comfortable doing it. I was always pushing myself to go beyond my comfort level. Hell, that was why I was in school.

But I was tired of being uncomfortable. Maybe it was acceptable—maybe even thrilling—to work at something that didn't make me uncomfortable all the time. Maybe I would end up doing research on food systems and then writing about them.

I didn't know.

As we drove down I-5 discussing what I would do for a project, I realized I was being too parochial. Who said I had to work with one of the organizations in the gorge where I lived?

I thought about my vision of a sustainable community: It was a place where the people were connected to each other and the environment. We didn't hurt Nature or each other. We had meaningful ceremonies and celebrations. We didn't waste. We didn't want. We had meaningful livelihoods. We grew, harvested, and cooked local foods. Our buildings were livable, beautiful, nontoxic. . . .

I could see all of this in my mind's eye. So how could I walk backward from that to see how my vision could come into being? What kind of organizations would have to collaborate to make my vision a reality?

In the first chapter of Weston's book, he writes, "Affirmative vision is crucial. Be emphatically, visibly, clearheadedly for something, and something that is worked out, widely compelling, and beautiful—not just against the problems or the powers-that-be of the moment" (Weston, 9).

It was so much more liberating thinking about what was possible instead of being weighed down by what felt impossible. It felt audacious to contemplate what kind of work I actually enjoyed now, at this time in my life, instead of trying to find something I thought I should do.

CERTIFIED

The word audacious comes from a Latin word meaning "to dare," to be bold. I was ready to be audacious again.

Or maybe for the first time?

I ended up coming up with a project where the Unitarian Church in Hood River, Oregon, would mentor foster teens. I called it Germination X: Foster Teens & Unitarians MiXing It Up!

Top of the World, Ma!

June

The second residency came and went uneventfully. For the third residency and for the final project I would do for school, I was supposed to create a seven minute podcast about a particular resource. I told the class I would probably do something about plants. I wanted to talk about listening to plants intuitively, but I wasn't sure how that would go over.

I had been spending more and more time with the plants. It was spring, after all, even though we could hardly tell. It had been cold and rainy ever since we had come home from Arizona. Some of us wondered if this had anything to do with the meltdown of the Japanese reactors after the earthquake and tsunami. Something felt off in our neck of the woods. The weather was awful, and people kept getting sick and not getting better for a long time.

The rivers were flooding, and I often went to the Doetsch Ranch at Beacon Rock State Park to walk and watch the river rise. Nettle grew up and around the old cottonwoods until they were nearly my height, with tiny blossoms hanging from the leaves like necklaces that had come undone. Bright green lemon balm grew close to the ground, just off the trail under the cottonwood trees. In shaded hollows here and there, tiny bleeding hearts grew up amongst wild geraniums and miner's lettuce. And the grass grew higher and higher, hiding tall, luscious, and elegant-looking comfrey plants—so deep green they were almost blue—and coltsfoot with their large multi-lobed leaves and odd-looking flower-heads growing up on a stalk that looked separate from the plant, its blossoms reminding me of an exploded fireworks display frozen in the sky of green.

I began talking to the plants again, especially those at the Ranch. And then I began talking *with* the plants. Or listening *to* the plants. I would stand next to a plant I didn't know and meditate with it, keeping my awareness open for images and thoughts. For one plant I "heard" that it was good for chest ailments. I also saw (in my mind's eye) that a lot was going on underneath—that the plants were actually a community of plants linked by what was hidden.

I went home and didn't try to find out what the plant was. But the next day I happened upon a drawing of the plant that looked just like the one I'd found in the field, and I saw it was Western coltsfoot. I did some research and found Western coltsfoot was used for coughs and lung ailments. And it grew from rhizomes, so many stems (and flowers) grew up from one creeping rhizome: like a community.

This happened again and again. I would meditate or hang out with the flower or plant and then go home and do research and find out that what I "heard" was correct.

In the midst of this, I made a podcast about the wonders of plants and how we should try to communicate with them. I didn't want to come off as some kind of flake, so I quoted lots of experts: Stephen Harrod Buhner, Timothy Lee Scot *(Invasive Plant Medicine),* Matthew Wood, and others. I spent the day making this seven minute podcast, and then I tried to put it out of my mind.

Only I kept thinking about the podcast. It had been a long and arduous year. Was I going to end it with this dull podcast about how cool plants were? It wasn't me. And it wasn't interesting.

So I made another podcast.

I still didn't like it.

Mario thought they were both great.

"But it's not me," I said.

Wasn't this last year all about changing me? All about me trying to find a more productive way to be in the world?

I kept thinking about the podcast.

Who was I? What did I enjoy doing?

I saw my life as a series of illnesses, at least my adult life. Yuck. That was no way to think about my life.

That was what had happened *to* me.

That wasn't who I was.

I was the person who wrote *Ruby's Imagine*. I was the one who opened my mind and imagination so that Ruby could tell me her beautiful story.

I was the person who wrote *Church of the Old Mermaids*. I was the one who sat in a little shack in the foothills of the foothills of the Rincon Mountains in Tucson and let Old Mermaids come up out of the wash and tell me their stories.

I was the person who made up a story about a magical carrot cake and told it to my food systems class as they sat spellbound through the whole tale.

I was the person who asked friends to bring found objects to a gathering of women, and then I held up each object, one at a time, and told an Old Mermaids tale based on the object.

I was a storyteller.

That was who I was.

A friend of mine told me once he was worried about what

would happen to me if I couldn't write or tell stories. He was afraid for my safety and sanity.

And then it happened to me. My mind went haywire for a time. The docs said I had multiple chemical sensitivities. I was allergic to the world. But I was not allergic to the world—I refused to believe that's even possible. Something did happen to me. For a while, I couldn't read or write. Even after I got better, my writing wasn't the same. I wasn't the same.

But that was then. See? I keep looking backward, seeing only these islands of illness and distress.

I made another podcast for my class. This time I told a story about a man called Thomas who was apprenticing to Old Mrs. Kelly to be a faery doctor.

It went something like this:

There are seven continents, this story is from the eighth continent.

This is the story of young Thomas who was sent to learn all that he could learn about the plants and herbs from Mrs. Kelly so he could come back to his village and be a faery doctor like Mrs. Kelly. Faery doctors were the best doctors because they got their wisdom from the faeries and from the plants.

Thomas was very good at identifying the plants, and he read every book he could find on plants. He listened to Mrs. Kelly, but he couldn't figure out how she did what she did. People would come to see her, she would listen to them, and then she would say to them, "Deep peace, deep peace." And she would give them some kind of remedy. Afterward she would ask, "Do you understand why I gave them this or that?" and Thomas would nod. But he didn't really understand. Mrs. Kelly started to wonder if she had made a mistake by allowing him to come apprentice with her.

One day Mrs. Kelly said to Thomas, "Have you heard the story of Thomas the Rhymer?"

Thomas shook his head. Mrs. Kelly was appalled. She couldn't understand how a young man like Thomas could have never heard the story of Thomas the Rhymer. And so she told him that Thomas the Rhymer went out to the forest and fell asleep under the hawthorn tree. And when he awakened, the Queen of Elfland was standing over him, wearing a beautiful green dress. She said, "Come, Thomas, and I will show you the world of nature," and so she took him into fairyland and there he learned all he could about nature.

And when he returned after seven years, he came into the village, and he was a great poet and a great bard. He was also a great healer, and he knew everything that could be known about herbs and other plants—and a little less and a little more.

Thomas listened to this story about Thomas the Rhymer, and he thought if he could learn from this man and learn the way Thomas the Rhymer had learned, he could leave this old woman and go back to his village. The next day he walked around Mrs. Kelly's village and asked people what they knew about Thomas the Rhymer. Everyone acknowledged they had heard the same story Mrs. Kelly had told him.

One man told Thomas that when Thomas the Rhymer came back, he had a book with him where he had written down everything that he learned in fairyland, including information about each and every plant and how they could cure people of all that ailed them. He had written down every remedy. And the man told Thomas he had heard Thomas the Rhymer's book was in the next village over.

Thomas went to Mrs. Kelly and told her he had to be away for a while. She gave him permission to go. He was underfoot most of the time anyway and didn't do her much good

So Thomas went to the next village to look for Thomas the Rhymer's book with all the secret knowledge in it. He asked around town, and people said the book used to be there, but it wasn't any longer. It was now in the next village over where they might have a museum. He went to the next village, and they pretty much told him the same thing. And he went to the next village and the next one.

Until finally, after he had gone to thirteen villages, someone actually took him up to an attic in an old house, got out a box, and said, "This is Thomas the Rhymer's book."

Thomas couldn't believe it was in this ordinary box. Shouldn't it be under glass? Shouldn't someone have written down all of these miraculous cures? He waited until the other man left, and he was alone. Then he put the book on his lap. He was so excited. Now he would know everything and he could leave that old woman and go back to his village and be a rich doctor.

He eagerly opened the book. The first page was blank. He flipped to the second page. It was blank, too. He quickly flipped through the book. Page after page was blank.

In fact, the whole book was blank.

He travelled back to the village and told Mrs. Kelly what had happened. He said he thought the story was a lie. There never was such a book with all the secrets of Thomas the Rhymer in it.

Mrs. Kelly laughed and said, "Of course, all the secrets of Thomas Rhymer were in that book. But they weren't meant for you. They were meant only for him. What you seek you will not find in any book. Remember that the plants are your neighbors, they are your companions, and you should treat them thus."

Thomas went out into the forest again and looked around at the plants and the trees. And he didn't feel anything or see anything. He sat on the ground, and he was very still. He breathed in and out. The sun climbed higher in the sky. Thomas felt sad, and he cried. Then he felt a breeze and he was happy. And he breathed in and out. And then suddenly it was as if he heard something. Not like you would hear a human voice. But he heard, "Deep peace, deep peace."

He looked right in front of him and saw this plant whose

green leaves looked like feet. He heard, "I am good for the chest." Thomas was so excited. He thanked the plant, and he thanked it again. He listened some more, and then he got up and ran back to Mrs. Kelly and told her what he had heard and felt.

Mrs. Kelly said, "I know this plant, and you have described it well. Your training has begun."

Mrs. Kelly and Thomas went out into the forest together again—and again and again. Thomas became the best apprentice that she had ever had. When people talked about Thomas, they said his secret was that every time he went out into the woods, he would stand or sit or be close to a plant and say, "Deep peace," and then the plant would begin to tell him all.

It may have been Thomas's deep peace blessing or it may have been that he treated the plants as his neighbors, finally and forever. Who knows? And this is true for each of us: We will find our own way.

I found a copy of one of Thomas's deep peace blessings in the attic, and I was able to read it, so I guess it was meant for me, and if you can hear it, it was meant for you.

It went something like this:

Deep peace I breathe into you,
Oh weariness here, oh ache here,
Deep peace of the soft white dove to you,
Deep peace of the quiet rain to you,
Deep peace of the ebbing wave to you,
Deep peace of the wildflowers to you,
Deep peace of the old forest to you,
Deep peace of the quiet earth to you,
Deep peace, deep peace.

I liked this podcast. It wasn't perfect, but it was me. (By the way, much of Thomas's Deep Peace blessing was based on an old Celtic blessing that was translated by Fiona MacLeod over a century ago.)

Soon it was time to go to my final residency of my final class.

Before I left I talked on the phone with the Family Member who had been having trouble with prescription drugs. I couldn't tell if she was using or not, but she was having some health problems. She told me about them, and I offered advice. Then she said she didn't want to be lectured, and she started to cry. I didn't think I was lecturing her. I knew she often thought she was doing everything wrong, and she believed everyone thought she was doing everything wrong. To be fair, I did think many of her decisions lately were self-destructive, and I didn't understand her thought process about many things.

But I was furious that she was accusing me of lecturing her. I felt like I had spent a good part of my life trying to save her from oncoming traffic. It only worked once. When she was a toddler, she had gone out into the road when I was supposed to watching her. I found her walking down the middle of the road, barefoot, in a diaper, while a truck barreled down the road toward her. I swooped her up in my arms and saved her.

Now she was her own person on her own journey. Now instead of saving her, I constantly felt like I was the one standing in traffic. And yet I wanted to save her. Or rather, I wanted her to be saved. I wanted her to be safe. If anything happened to her, it would be too difficult for our family to bear.

But now I wanted to scream at her as she told me not to lecture her. I wanted to scream at her to get her shit together because she was fucking up her life. Instead, I apologized. I knew it was foolish to argue with her if she was using. If she wasn't using, she was obviously feeling vulnerable and me screaming at her wasn't going to help. I told her I was just trying to help by giving her advice based on my experience.

Hah!

I got off the phone and talked to Mario about what had happened. He said, "Most of the time people just want to talk. They want someone to listen to them."

I rolled my eyes. "I hate talking on the phone," I said, "so I'm not going to just sit there and be held captive while someone dumps their crap on me. Do they want to solve the problem or just talk about it?"

He shrugged. Clearly he understood her point of view better than mine.

"Why would they call me if they didn't want my advice?" I asked.

"Because you're family," he said.

I didn't get it. Of course, I didn't tell my family about my life. I kept most of my business private. My hopes, fears, dreams weren't for my family. My family knew less about my life than people who read my blog. My family didn't understand my life, and for the most part, they didn't care. At least, that was what I had gathered from experience.

I didn't really understand why my sister got upset with me, but I told myself I would try to be better at just listening when people called me. I wouldn't give my advice unless asked. And I certainly wasn't going to talk about my life.

Before Mario and I left for Seattle, I suggested to Mario that we look at our relationship and see if there were some things we needed to change. We were celebrating our thirtieth wedding anniversary this month, so I thought it was a good idea to take stock.

Sometimes I am a complete and utter idiot.

If it ain't broke, why fix it?

Almost immediately, Mario and I stopped getting along. We were suddenly out of sync—or as if we were speaking two different languages. Then we were stuck in a car together for four hours. Fortunately we gave a friend of ours a ride to Tacoma.

CERTIFIED

That took the burden off of us having to talk to one another for part of the trip.

I hadn't been able to get us a room at the place we usually stayed, so I rented the Quaker House rooms again. Mario and I were going to be stuck in a tiny bedroom about the size of our bathroom for three days. Three days. I was not looking forward to this weekend. I can't describe exactly what was off between us: I was cranky, and he was nonresponsive, which always pissed me off. And, of course, I felt like shit most of the time.

After we dropped our stuff off at the Quaker House, we decided to walk to the Medicinal Herb Garden. The city seemed especially noisy on this Friday afternoon. As each car roared by us, I felt like I was being slapped. My nervous system started to overload. The wind blew dust up all around us as we walked. We got to the garden, but it seemed noisy, too. We didn't stay long. On the way back to the Quaker House, I held tightly to Mario's hand and tried to shield myself from all the noise and activity. I kept my head down and trusted him to lead me back to safety.

Finally, gratefully, we arrived back at the cool quiet Quaker House. It was such a relief. I sat quietly on my bed, wondering how I was ever going to survive in this world. My school year was almost over. I thought I'd be all cured this year. That had been my goal. It had been my goal for many years.

This line of thinking usually got me spiraling down into depression.

Not this time.

I looked up at Mario and said, "You know, I think it's normal to feel overwhelmed when there's too much noise and pollution and activity. I'm not odd. I'm not sick. I am experiencing a natural reaction to an unnatural state."

That's right.

It wasn't me.

I was natural.

Still, this natural person curled up into a fetal position on the bed. I didn't want to go anywhere. Mario found a menu for Araya's Place, a vegan Thai restaurant that had gluten-free food. It was only a few blocks away, so he left to get us takeout.

I put the movie *Under the Tuscan Sun* in my computer and watched it until I was feeling better. Then I got up and went out to meet Mario. I grinned when I caught a glimpse of him walking down the sidewalk in the near distance, holding a takeout bag. We met and walked back to the Quaker House. We set up plates in our tiny room. Then we had some of the best food I could ever remember eating: delicious rice noodles and spicy vegetables, brown and white rice, and tofu and vegetables.

Later that night as Mario and I lay in our separate twin beds, I said, "OK, in permaculture we try to take problems and make them the solution. What could we do about the freeway that's above this whole neighborhood?"

It felt better to think about solutions than to focus on what wasn't working.

We began talking about what was possible, and then we decided to think about what was supposedly impossible. In Portland, they had removed a freeway (Harbor Drive) to build Tom McCall Waterfront Park and this had helped transform the city. Together, Mario and I imagined the nearby freeway disappearing. We imagined the stress lifting from the bodies of those who lived in these neighborhoods where they were bombarded with the constant sound of tires moving over pavement, an unpleasant white noise that never seemed to abate. In our imaginations, the noise disappeared. The city was more livable, the people more resilient.

In our imagination is where better worlds always begin.

As we talked to one another, in our separate beds, Mario and I began to fall into step with one another again.

After a while, Mario fell asleep, and the light came on

outside and brightened the room. I could hear someone talking, too. Normally, I would have felt like this was an intrusion. How dare "they" turn on the light? How dare they disturb my rest? Then I thought about all the times I had travelled in Europe. If something happened there to disturb my sleep, I just felt like it was part of the adventure of travelling. If I heard people talking, it was part of the charm of the place.

Why couldn't I do that here? Why did I always take things personally?

So I became charmed by the light and the sound of voices.

Just like that.

Eventually the light went off, and the voices went away.

Quiet ensued. I was charmed by the quiet.

I fell asleep smiling.

The next day, I went to class at school for the first half of the day. For the second half, we all met at the teacher's house, just as we had a year ago. We listened to two community activists talk for a while, and then we listened to each other's podcasts. Everyone was clever and inventive: They talked about resources like hugs, playing in nature, coffee, trash, dandelions. And then the instructor played my podcast.

It seemed as though you could hear a pin drop as they listened. I couldn't tell if they liked it. It was so different from when I'm LIVE reading or telling a story or talking to a group. When it was over, I got lots of kudos. The teacher asked what I learned from the experience. I got choked up. I said, "I learned I am a storyteller. I haven't been able to make a living from my stories yet, but that's who I am."

I was glad I had done it my way.

Cue Frank Sinatra.

After class, the teacher invited us to stay for potluck. I remembered the potluck from a year ago. No one had talked to me. Not even the teacher. The teacher's parents had talked with me, and that had been kind. Sadly, the father—the one who had lent me his AAA card so that I could get a locksmith to come out and unlock my car (since I'd locked my keys in the trunk)—had died unexpectedly only a month earlier.

I hadn't brought anything for the potluck, plus I didn't actually want to stay, so I hugged a few of the people I had had classes with all year. And then I left.

I got into the car and drove out of west Seattle toward the University district. My year of schooling was almost over. I just had to write a final reflection. Then fini.

I got to the Quaker House where we met up with a friend, and then we walked to Araya's for dinner. Somehow the onslaught of traffic and noise didn't seem to bother me as much today. Perhaps it was because I was in the company of my friend.

We had a good dinner and conversation.

The next morning Mario and I got up very early and walked a couple of blocks to the Portage Bay Cafe for breakfast. I had scrambled tofu and potatoes. After, we drove north from Seattle toward Bastyr University. Once we got off the expressway, we drove down shaded windy streets and then down a long drive until we came out of the woods and onto the open sunny campus of this small university.

It was about 9:00 a.m. on a Sunday morning, so hardly anyone was around. We parked by the main building. To the left of this building, a short distance away, was what looked like student housing. In-between the student housing and the main building was the medicinal herb garden.

I got out of the car and took a deep breath. I felt instantly relieved, as though I had just come home. It was so quiet and peaceful after being in the city. I loved it instantly. I wanted to teach here. Or live here. Maybe I should have gone to school at Bastyr. All sorts of thoughts went through my head when I first got out of the car. My acupuncturist, Jasmine, had told me about

CERTIFIED

Bastyr some months earlier, but the time and the weather had never been right. Today was perfect.

We left the car behind and walked across the campus to the Medicinal Herb Garden. At first it looked smaller than the one at the University of Washington. As I walked around these circles of medicinal herbs, I began to feel as though I was in the middle of an enormous garden.

They had planted different beds of medicinal herbs according to which part of the body they healed: brain, nervous system, respiratory system, etc. They had an elemental garden with four beds, each one based on a particular element. They had Ayurvedic herbs in one bed and Chinese medicinal herbs in another. They had a "shade garden" and inside it were "at risk" plants they were nurturing.

I was in awe. Now this was a medicinal herb garden. I first heard about "plague gardens" outside hospitals and clinics when I read a biography of 17th century scientific illustrator Maria Sibylla Merian *(Chrysalis: Maria Sibylla Merian and the Secrets of Metamorphosis* by Kim Todd). When I read the words "plague garden," a chill went up my spine. I knew that one day I would write a book called *Plague Garden.* This was what my plague garden would be like.

We stayed at the gardens for a long time. The longer I was there, the longer I wanted to stay. I took off my shoes and socks and walked along the reflexology path. When I was a kid, I had spent most of my life barefoot and outside. Now my soles were soft and vulnerable.

Eventually Mario and I headed home. We stopped in Tacoma to pick up our friend. Thankfully the long drive home was uneventful, and we arrived back safely.

I wrote my final reflection the next day. A day or two later, I got sick again. I wondered why. Maybe I hadn't honored the

Dragon of Seattle enough? Or maybe I had eaten too much. I didn't know. I was frustrated.

I wasn't going to give up, though. I went back on an anti-inflammatory diet. Since my mother died, I had been eating more sweets than I usually did. Now I cut out sweets completely. Ate more protein and less carbs. I started meditating more regularly and doing breathing exercises. I turned off the TV. No more crime shows. No more murders.

A few days later, the weekend after we got back from Seattle, I attended a workshop on Celtic Shamanism and Druid Wisdom Tales taught by Tom Cowan. It was a small group, and several people from my two-year Celtic Shamanism program attended, too. Even though I was practically hacking up a lung half the time, I enjoyed myself immensely.

A friend once told me that I needed to find my tribe. When that happened, all would be well. I felt as though I was with my peers—with my tribe—at the workshop.

As I wandered the grassy labyrinth in the meadow with several of my friends, I thought about my classmates up in Seattle. Were they part of my tribe? They were certainly people who believed in being active members of their communities. They were working toward a sustainable and resilient world. I liked that. That was my plan, too. I didn't know any of them well enough to know whether they were part of my tribe.

This meadow, the birds overhead, the cottonwoods along the shore of the creek, the angelica growing in another field, the deer that grazed, hidden, in the tall grass, and the people walking with me in the labyrinth were part of my tribe. They were committed to their relationships with the unseen—and nature.

I listened to stories all weekend. And I drummed and rattled. Told stories. Tom quoted Thomas Berry who said "we are the place the Earth dreams." I liked that.

I came into the main meeting room one morning and found

an antler rattle on my chair. It was a gift from one of my Celtic brothers. The gesture brought me to tears, especially after I learned he had found the antler in the woods while hiking barefoot. Then he had made it into a rattle himself.

The rattle held significance for me for another reason, too. Despite being under great stress and not feeling well at the time, two months earlier I had decided to take a 10-week Sound Healing course. Before I originally started back to school, I had clients and did healing work. I had put all of this on hold once I started school.

I hadn't stopped doing the healing work just because I went back to school. It was also because I doubted what I was doing. I could see that I helped some people, but I didn't help others. Primarily, I didn't help myself. To me, if I couldn't heal myself, what good were any of my healing abilities? How real or efficacious were the techniques I used if I was still ill?

When this sound healing class came up, I thought maybe it was just what I needed to get well. I was always desperately looking for an answer. I was desperately looking for wellness. I already did some sound healing with my clients, but once again, I thought an "expert" could give me clues so I could do it better.

So I signed up.

The actual ten week class was problematic for many reasons that I won't go into. But it had its good moments. During one journey (a shamanic meditation), we went on to find out about the sound instrument we were supposed to make, one of my helpers told me someone would give me an antler. I remember thinking, "No one I know is going to give me an antler." One night I dreamed someone gave me a rattle. When I awakened from the dream I decided to make the rattle I was given in the dream, so that's what I did. I used a rosemary branch for the handle, a friend gave me rabbit fur for decoration, and I bought some elk hide for the head of the rattle. I put in black beans and yellow corn for the rattle part. It was beautiful, the sound was lovely, and I took it around Doetsch Ranch and let all the plants bless it.

Now, three days before our final sound healing class and our public community healing, my Celtic brother gave me an antler. Not only an antler but an antler rattle. I knew I would use it in the community healing.

It was a beautiful weekend. I slept well. I felt nourished by the place and the people. I went home quite happy and content.

The following day, I had an urge to go to the Grotto, a 62-acre Catholic shrine and botanical garden in Portland. I wasn't sure why I wanted to go. I missed my dad, and I had taken my mom and dad to the Grotto years earlier. I took my camera, and Mario and I went up to the garden, situated above the church. The rhododendrons were in bloom, and I took lots of photos. We wandered around the trails of this semi-wild, semi-manicured acreage, and suddenly we saw a labyrinth sign. We had never seen a labyrinth at the Grotto before.

We turned down the trail and walked to a labyrinth. It was off away from the rest of the gardens, tucked beneath tall old Doug firs. The area was semi-dark, secluded, faery-like. It was a Chartres labyrinth, unlike the more classical labyrinth at Still Meadow where the workshop had been. This one was made from stones or bricks that looked like they had each been fashioned by hand.

I took a deep breath and stepped onto the path. I walked around every bend and curve, walked down each straightaway. How many years ago had I gotten sick and dizzy and thought of myself as the Minotaur trying to find my way out of a labyrinth that felt more like a maze than a path in and out? I had walked an outdoor labyrinth at Grace Cathedral in San Francisco. I had walked on the indoor labyrinth at the Trinity Episcopal Cathedral in Portland. Mario and I had made a labyrinth on the Oregon beach once and walked it until the tide washed it away. In Santa Fe, we had gone to the labyrinth by the folk museum in the dead of night and walked it. (That was so much fun!) I had walked the labyrinth at Still Meadow many times over the years. Whenever I reached the center of it, I felt as though I were home.

Now I walked this new labyrinth with Mario. A couple of other people joined us. I liked that. I liked being with other people on the labyrinth. But none of them finished it: They all walked straight out once they reached the center. As I followed the curves, I saw a snail also "walking" the labyrinth. She who carried her house on her back. I looked down at her beautiful spiral and thought, "Yes, yes, yes. Everything is the same." When I began walking, she was going one way and then eventually she went the other way, out of the labyrinth.

When I got to the center, I felt the presence of all my guides. I was always nourished by what was invisible in the world. And it may be what was invisible in the world was also what plagued me. At the center, I meditated with my guides, and then I walked the curves of the labyrinth until I reached the end.

Then I took off my shoes and socks, and I walked it again.

I was giddy by the time I left.

The next night, I was in the center of a large room with seven other people. We were surrounded by a circle of thirty or more people. Our teacher had honored the directions and told the community how we would proceed. Now we were preparing to do a sound healing on a client who was on the massage table.

We began by making sound. We used our voices. We used the instruments we had made: rattles, whistles, feathers and bells. We used drums, cymbals, bells (big and tiny), singing bowls (crystal and metal). We made pleasing sounds at first, then cacophonous noise, then soothing sounds. We worked in concert, in harmony and disharmony.

We did this for three hours, for one client after another. It felt otherworldly. It felt profound and communal. This surprised me because I had not connected with this group of people. They all belonged to a particular shamanic school in Portland, everyone except me and a friend of mine who had recommended the course. They all knew one another and I was, once again, a stranger. I had known the teacher for several years. We weren't buddies or anything close. It didn't matter. Somehow we all came together and did the work.

Maybe that was what community was: doing the work whether you liked or connected with the people or not. That wasn't my idea of community, but maybe that was all we got some of the time. Other times, we got our soul brothers and sisters, like at the Druid Wisdom Tales workshop I had attended a few days earlier.

I used my deer rattle during this community sound healing. As I held it in my hand, I thought of my Celtic brother who had gifted it to me. I felt ancient and wise and connected to the spine and bloodstream of the world.

A couple of days later, I drove to Portland by myself and went to the grotto again. This time I took with me the rattle I had made and the antler rattle my brother had gifted to me. I walked the labyrinth first with the rattle I had made. Then I walked the labyrinth with bare feet, gently holding and shaking the antler rattle. Then I walked it a third time, silently.

Each time I walked the labyrinth, I felt as though I were on the back of a serpent, not just on stones on the ground.

At home again I felt like something was coming to a head. Something was changing. My breathing seemed worse rather than better. What was going on? I thought of my year in school. What had I accomplished?

I had survived it.

I had survived a very difficult year with my family.

I looked at almost everything a little differently than I had

CERTIFIED

a year ago. I knew more change happened in the world when people were inspired, not when they were bludgeoned with depressing facts. I knew more about the food system than I had known before—and I thought I'd known a lot. I knew a lot about permaculture. I could probably even design gardens and like doing it, as long as my gardens told stories. They had to nourish body and soul.

Beauty had to be a part of the equation.

If there even was an equation.

I sat at my desk one day and looked at all my certificates. I thought about all my degrees. I was an educated woman in the liberal and healing arts.

And yet, I was still so un-easy. I still gasped for breath.

Something else was going on with me. With the world. Would I ever know what? I had spent twenty-five years trying to get healthy.

Was my life a wasted life?

I wanted more.

My cough held on. My breathing was ragged.

This was ridiculous.

I stopped using my inhaler. I gasped for breath, but I continued doing breathing exercises. I told myself I could breathe, I could breathe.

I kept hearing this small voice in my head getting louder, "You've learned all these things, now use them on YOURSELF."

I began giving myself pep talks. I listened to the plants and took remedies. I asked my dreams for answers.

Another voice said, "You've done all this before. It didn't work then, and it won't work now."

Another voice said, "That was the past. Quit getting stuck in the past."

One day, I walked partway up Wind Mountain on my own.

It's a steep elevation. I talked to the poison oak at the beginning of the trail and asked for safe passage. I asked the Spirits and Beings of the place for safe passage. It was difficult, but I went to the first plateau without using my inhaler. And I got a healing. The Spirit said, "There, now go home and forget about it."

I slipped and fell once going down, but I wasn't hurt.

Five days later, Mario and I decided to walk to the top of Wind Mountain.

We passed by the poison oak with a whispered blessing. Then up we went. Mario went ahead of me. I had to stop a lot. My chest was tight, but I didn't want to take any medication. So I went slowly. Up we went. I felt like I was climbing Everest. Where was my oxygen?

Up we went. Then rested. Drank water. Walked.

I whispered to the mountain and the Beings of the Mountain every step of the way.

I wondered if I would drop dead of a heart attack. Or maybe my lungs would close down.

At least I was out of doors. At least I had my feet on Mother Earth.

I missed my own mother. I missed my dad.

My mom used to run. She had asthma, too. She wanted to be well more than anything. She never got well.

But maybe I could.

That would be all right, wouldn't it? If I got well.

Up.

I didn't know if I could make it.

It was so hard.

One time I was bent over gasping for breath, and I noticed a purple flower. Its leaves looked like it was in the lupine family. I talked to it for a bit. I knew "lupine" meant wolf, and I suddenly got a vision of a mother wolf, close to the ground. She could breathe.

CERTIFIED

She could breathe.
Yes, I could be like that wolf.
I could breathe.
I caught my breath, and I walked.
Up the mountain I went.
Over three talus fields.
I was a wolf.
A flower.
A breeze.
I was me.
Around the corner.
I was at the top.

Almost. I was surrounded by bright green ferns overgrowing the path. All around me trees rose. Doug firs? I didn't notice. In the distance, 1,200 feet below, the Columbia River ran swollen and brown, near flood stage from our above average rainfall. The river curved west, past Beacon Rock, heading toward the ocean.

We heard sticks breaking, like how bears do in the woods to let you know where they are. So Mario broke sticks, too. And then a woman emerged from the green. She smiled and said hello and walked by us. We walked a few feet more and saw a man coming down from the top. He was grinning. Happy.

He stopped to talk. He had never been before. They had left an offering. He was so excited. I listened to him talk about his life. He asked us our names, and then I asked him his name. "Benny," he said.

I smiled. I had a character named Benjamin in all of my novels (or nearly all). I wasn't sure how it had started, but now the name was a kind of good luck charm.

We said our good-byes, and the man started to walk away. I said, "Is your wife's totem a bear by any chance?"

"It's mine," he said, "and we're pretty much joined at the hip."

"So it was your bearness we sensed," I said.

He smiled and then said goodbye.

Mario went and stood by one of the old trees on the west side of the mountain. I continued through the brush up to the top of the mountain, where no trees or brush grew. I stood at the top of a large talus field.

I had made it.

I had walked to the top of Wind Mountain without using any medication.

It was probably the first time in twenty-some years that I hadn't had to use medication to walk so far and so high.

It was one of the highlights of my life so far. And it had been one of the most difficult things I had ever done. Nearly every step of the way I wondered if I was going to die.

Now I was ecstatic.

And a little out of breath.

I was at the top of a mountain where the indigenous people of this area used to come for their vision quests.

I wondered if they still came.

I held my arms up to the east and thanked the Spirits and Beings of the East. The river curved away to the east. Then I held my arms up to the south, where most of my view was blocked by the tops of the trees, but I could see the blue sky. I thanked the Spirits and Beings of the South.

I turned to the west and looked into the tangle of trees and brush, and I thanked the Spirits and Beings of the West. Finally I turned to the north. In the distance the hillsides were dark green with Doug firs. And further in the distance, I could see a mountaintop. I couldn't see enough to tell which mountain it was, but we figured it was Mount Adams. I thanked the Spirits and Beings of the North.

CERTIFIED

And I thanked what is above, below, and all around. I thanked the Mountain and all who lived in this Place.

Alone on this mountaintop—well, free of human companionship at least—I held my arms up, took a deep full breath, and cried out, "Top of the world, Ma!"

I left an offering of salmon. Mario came and stood with me for a while. Then another couple arrived. They sat and talked on a cellphone.

Mario and I said our goodbyes to the mountain, and then we began a mindful descent.

Healing

I thought I went back to school for noble reasons. I wanted to figure out new ways to save the world because my ways weren't working.

It had been one of the worst years of my life.

It had also been one of the most amazing years of my life.

I thought I had returned to school to acquire new skills. Maybe I had gone back to school because I had always excelled in school. Maybe I had wanted to do something I was good at again. I was so tired of failing.

Maybe I thought it would be comfortable. I could get back into the mainstream of life after years of illness. After years of being an edge dweller, where I talked to trees, plants, clouds, the wind, the air. Where I drummed and rattled and asked the plants for answers.

Only this time, I hadn't excelled at school. Or maybe I had. They didn't give out grades, so even if I had excelled I wouldn't know it. I did well in my classes, but it didn't change anything. It didn't mean anything. No one was praising me. No one was telling me how great I was.

Did that mean I craved attention and approval?

CERTIFIED

Probably.

Oh my.

In the end, I didn't feel any better about myself because of my year in school. I knew so much already. That was one of the things I learned. About certain topics—like sustainability, green living, etc.—I was a font of knowledge. A font of wisdom, even, maybe.

I went to school looking for a way to heal the world because then I would be healed. Fixed. Put back together again like Humpty Dumpty after his great fall.

I thought it would direct me back into the world again. Propel me into the world.

Instead I began talking in earnest to plants again.

For so many years I had been fearful of being labeled New Age. (Still makes me shudder.) I didn't want to be considered some kind of flake who didn't understand science or logic. Because I did understand science and logic. I might be different, but I was good different.

But I had to face it. Essentially I was one of those people. I wasn't a flake and neither were they. Something had happened to our culture, or our human world, when we turned away from nature. Things got lopsided. Things got very dangerous. Things got sick.

When we stopped listening to the trees, we lost our ancient wisdom. When we stopped hearing the plants, we lost our Earth medicine. When we stopped thinking like a mountain, we lost our ability to be still and grounded. When we began ignoring the unseen, our world began unraveling. When we stopped listening to our dreams, the world became a nightmare.

We stopped hearing and telling stories.

Muriel Rukeyser said, "The universe is made of stories, not of atoms."

I had been trying to save the world and my family since I was a young girl.

Can we save the world if we can't save ourselves?

I've been in for repairs for too much of my life.

I ain't broken no more. At least not this moment.

Yesterday a lupine flower who turned into a wolf helped me climb a mountain.

That's the truth.

As I know it.

When I took a deep breath on top of the mountain yesterday, I felt as though I was breathing in myself.

I was becoming full of my one true self.

I am full of myself.

At least that's what I'm hoping I'm full of.

It's all an adventure, isn't it?

I wish you blessings on all your adventures.

May it be so.

Appendix

Here's "The Wild Keeper," an essay I wrote for my Special Topics class and included in my book *Under the Tucson Moon*.

The Wild Keeper

What if we each pledged to care for a plot of land? It could be a square foot, the footprint of the place where we live, a piece of property we own, or a park we love. We would care for these pieces, these plots, these Earthly parcels, like we would care for our fingers or our arms or our legs: We would recognize that it is all a part of us, and as the land is cared for, so are we.

Sometimes I close my eyes and I can see all these pieces of land like pieces of a quilt. We could link them all up, put them all together, and then we would have one beautiful quilt of the world. It's already there, this quilt, so perhaps our jobs—as caretakers—is to repair the torn pieces, re-stitch those places where the thread has come out, and clear away the debris.

Because I'm a writer, I often see the world in metaphor—the land is like our body, the land is a quilt, the land is our mother. But I feel the world in my bones, too. I breathe the world in and out. I take off my shoes and I step on the grass, on the dirt, on the earth, and feel my soles against the soul of the world. I feel the Earth—Nature—beneath my feet like an ocean wave, and I know I should grab a surfboard and enjoy the wild ride.

Sometimes I feel the Wild pulsing in my own soul, and I know it is Nature speaking to me, through me. I feel as though my creative force and my passion for the world is Nature working her art through me: I am her art piece.

I like finding others who are not like-minded but like-souled. Is that a word? I crave the wild. I don't do extreme sports. I'm not a good camper. I don't climb mountains. I have a need to be out of doors, but it's not to prove anything to myself or anyone else. It is like drinking water or eating food or breathing air. It is as necessary as all of those things. I feel myself shrinking and changing when I cannot be in a place where the wild things roam.

Years ago, I heard that jaguars were coming back into the American Southwest. Two of them had been photographed. I began to dream of jaguars. They were always powerful, frightening, and alluring. I felt as though this cat was speaking to me, as though these jaguars meant something to me, personally, as well as to the world. I wanted to write about them. I began talking to people about jaguars.

I wanted to find people who understood about the wild.

And so I found Sergio Avila, a biologist who was working for Sky Island Alliance. One year we talked about how to protect and conserve the jaguars in the United States. One year we talked about the death of one of the jaguars after it was captured and collared. Sergio and I spoke a common language about nature.

I found other people who lived on the land and understood the ways of the wild, too. I talked to ranchers and hunters and biologists and conservationists. Many of them were trying to save and protect their lands and their livelihoods. All of them wanted to make certain the land was viable for the wild creatures, in one way or another. They didn't all agree with one another. Some felt sad, angry, and betrayed by what happened after the collared jaguar died.

But that is another story for another day. I will piece together that story soon. Now I want to think about the living wild.

One day when Sergio and I talked about the wild world, he told me about Carlos Robles Elías, a rancher in Sonora, Mexico. He had 10,000 acres and he was dedicating it to wildlife conservation. A wild jaguar and several ocelots had been photographed on the ranch. You must speak with him, Sergio suggested; he could be the hero of the book you are writing. I felt the hair stand up on the back of my neck again, just as it had when I first learned about the jaguar.

And so one day, I was in a truck with Carlos and my husband, and we were driving down windy Sonoran roads. The truck shook from a bad tire, but we drove toward El Aribabi Conservation Ranch and we talked about conservation. I scribbled in my notebook while Carlos talked, and I looked up occasionally at the landscape around us. It looked familiar. Had I been here before?

Carlos spoke passionately about conservation. He wasn't certain how he had come to his views, but he thought it had a great deal to do with his older brother who would talk to him about nature. Carlos had moved the cattle off of his ranch. He wanted to make his ranch a paradise for wildlife and show his neighbors how it worked. They were waiting to see if he would be successful at it. Could it be economically feasible?

I told Carlos that in my country if someone owned 10,000 acres they were rich. He said he was not rich. He was struggling. He wanted to make enough money to have a normal life with his wife, Martha, and their three children. "I don't want a Hummer," he said. "Or anything like that. I want a normal life."

And on his piece of land, his parcel of Earth, he wanted to make a home for the wild. He wanted to make his conservation ranch viable so that "wildlife would have a home forever." He believed the most important thing was a massive education program, about trash, about conservation, about wildlife. Now people throw trash on the ground and don't even think about it, he said. When someone sees a snake, they think they have to kill it.

"If we educate the children about the snake," he said, "then they won't feel they have to kill it and they will keep it alive."

He has school children come out to the ranch and play in the stream. He wants them to know what it is like to be in nature.

I nodded and wrote as he talked. It always surprises me that people need to be taught about nature, that they don't feel an innate connection with the environment. It was, I supposed, like teaching people they had a heart. They couldn't see it, but it kept them alive.

As we drove, Carlos spoke about his ranch. He had over thirty protected, threatened, and endangered species on the land, including a jaguar and several ocelots. He had over 180 species. He told me the jaguar came up to his land to live because it was a quiet place, a protected place.

Carlos pointed out areas along the route where the land had been overgrazed. It wasn't just that too many cattle were bad for nature, he said; it was that the cowboys would kill anything.

CERTIFIED

They saw something wild, and they'd shoot it, especially mountain lions.

Soon we arrived at the ranch. We went through the gate and passed by huge old cottonwood trees. They looked like old naked dancers, reaching up to the sky or off to the side to stretch. They looked like guardians, too, and I waved. I'd like to talk with them. What had they seen over the years?

Below the ranch house a stream wove its way through a copse of cottonwood trees. Or maybe it was the other way around. The cottonwoods were drawn to the water. Something profound and glorious about water in the desert, always.

Carlos took us out onto the ranch. He drove slowly through a mesquite forest. Several of the mesquite trees were huge and hundreds of years old. Mesquite roots go very deep—they know how many secrets are buried in the dirt—and I wondered how far down the roots of these ancient trees went. Some of the trees were much younger and had several small trunks instead of one large one. They had come up after Carlos's grandfather bulldozed the area 40 years earlier and planted grass for the cattle.

We drove on the ridge tops, following the line of the hills, looking down at the grasslands. I thought for certain we would see a mountain lion in these blond grasses. I could feel them all around us. This place was more wild than any African savannah. More desolate. And beautiful.

Eventually we stopped on one of the ridges to wait for Sergio, who had just arrived at the ranch house. Below us were the hilly grasslands, dotted with yucca. Around us in all directions were the ancient mountains, slouching into the earth, their jaggedness rounded off from age or experience. On many of the nearby slopes, we could see wildlife tracks going through the tall grass. Carlos pointed to a peak just beyond: That was where they had photographed the jaguar.

We were in jaguar country.

I loved listening to Carlos talk. He knew every inch of these wild lands. And they were wild lands, make no mistake about that. It was a harsh landscape filled with wild life: rattlesnakes, mountain lions, bears, bobcats, foxes, ocelots, and a least one jaguar. This wasn't the prairie where you'd take a snooze on the soft grass. This wasn't a temperate forest fairy land. This was harsh dry country. It made the hairs on the back of my neck stand up. It made my soles sweat. It was so silent and majestic; I felt my soul settle into my body and relax.

Take a deep breath. This is the wild. This is where you are most at home.

And this man Carlos was protecting this wild place. He was restoring the land so that it was a good home—so that wild life and people could thrive. People need wild places. Children need to play in wild streams. Men and women need to hear wolves howl and coyotes yip. People need to be connected to the wild. The soul's true nature is unleashed when it hears, senses, sees, dances the song of the wild.

I'm sure of it.

I knew Carlos only a few hours and I knew this: He felt the beat of the land in his heart. In his soul. Later, Carlos would say of Sergio (or Sergio would say of Carlos) that they understood each other because their common language was nature.

That is my language, too.

Later Mario told me we had been on the windy road to the ranch before. That was why it had seemed familiar to me. Several years earlier, I had felt the need to go to Mexico, to go out into the countryside, into the desert. I knew something awaited me there. I thought it was a home, a parcel of land that was calling to me. I wasn't sure. We drove down the road for a long while. We stopped the car and I stood in the middle of the road and listened to the silence. I breathed deeply and wondered what had drawn me to this place. Now all these years later I was back—only this time, I had someone who opened the gate for me, who invited me in.

Invited me to this wild place.

When Sergio arrived, we continued on the road, this time going down into the canyon. We saw a huge buck running up one ridge. The buck stopped and watched us for a time and then continued on his journey and we continued on ours. We drove to the canyon floor and stopped by two buildings in progress, one made from adobe, the other from local rocks. Carlos planned on using four energy sources for these buildings once they were completed: solar, wind, hydropower, and pedal power.

We walked past the houses, through the tall grass, and into the empty stream bed. Small leaves crunched beneath our feet. This was a dry place. The boy scouts had been out last summer doing restoration work in the stream. They put large rocks at various places in the stream to slow the water that came cascading down the canyon during the rainy season. This would help prevent erosion and allow the water time to soak into the ground and raise the water table. As we stood in the peaceful stream bed, we could feel the difference in temperature even though the creek was empty now. It was noticeably cooler. Since the scouts had done this work, the level of the water in Carlos's well had risen.

Carlos wanted to show everyone that many of these kinds of changes could be made quite simply. The boy scouts had done this restoration work in one day. Actions = results.

We talked about many things. Sometimes Carlos spoke in Spanish and Sergio translated. I often understood the gist of what he was saying, and always I understood the passion. He wanted his ranch to be a working model for sustainability. He wanted scientific research done here. He wanted a conservation school to be built here.

But right now, it was difficult for him to make a living off the ranch. Something had to change. They needed to get some kind of income so they could keep the land wild, and so they could keep doing research and restoration work.

I understood this dilemma. How to live in this world and do the right work.

Why did keeping the wild wild always come down to economics? Why was so much of life like that? Some old European towns used to keep a portion of their towns and communities wild. No one owned this land. Everyone cared for this land. It was where the ancient trees grew and the wild animals lived. When the conquerors came, they always decimated these commons and cut down the ancestor trees in an effort to destroy what the community held most dear.

Who are the conquerors now? We are decimating our own commons. Is it because we can't feel the wild beating in our own hearts?

The four of us drove back to the ranch and had lunch under the portico along with several researchers from a Sonoran university. As I sat at the table eating, I wondered how Carlos could keep this land wild. I imagined desert gardens all around the ranch house—permaculture gardens. I imagined tables and chairs under the portico and people visiting from all over and paying for the privilege of being there. I imagined trails leading from the house to other places on the ranch. If gardens and trails were created near the house, all kinds of workshops could happen here. Writers and artists would want to stay at the house or go further out to be alone.

Or people could come who wanted to research or explore. Archaeological teams did that all the time: They charged volunteers to work for them. Couldn't something like that happen at the ranch?

It seemed like this place could become a sanctuary for humans as well as other wild life. A place to connect with the outer wild life and one's own inner wild life.

Carlos was trying to keep the wild wild. Sergio was doing that, too.

That was what I tried to do, in my way. With my wild words.

Not long ago, Carlos told us, someone caught an ocelot on their land and brought it to him to put on his land. He said no. When he told us this story, I said, "That's because you don't want this to be a zoo. You want this ranch to be a kind of template so that others can do that same thing on their own land." He wasn't a zoo keeper. He was a *wild* keeper. He wanted to make his land wild and demonstrate how others could do the same.

Later, Mario and I wandered around the house and then went down to the stream while Carlos and José changed a bulging tire on the truck. I liked being on the land. I liked my soles against this earth. Mario and I watched the sunlight hit the tops of the cottonwoods as the sun began to set. It was so quiet here. I felt peace in this wild place.

Still later, Carlos drove us back to the border. We talked of many things on the drive. When he stopped to drop us off, I shook his hand and thanked him for a wonderful day. Then Mario and I got out of the truck and walked across the border to our car. We drove for an hour or so to Tucson and stopped into a restaurant for a late dinner. We ordered too much food. I ate too much. I missed the land already. I missed the easy wild day.

I had to remember that the wild was always in me. I didn't have a parcel of land to care for. I had me. I had my words. Maybe in some way, that helps the world. I hoped Carlos could keep his land wild, for his sake, but also for the sake of the world. We will always need wild places and wild keepers.

Bibliography

(Since this is not a scholarly book, and it is an unconventional book, my citations and bibliography are also unconventional. These are some of the books and websites I mentioned in the book.)

Buhner, Stephen Harrod. Any of his books.

Conroy, Pat. *The Prince of Tides*. Any edition.

Hemenway, Toby. *Gaia's Garden*. Chelsea Green Publishing Company: 2009.

Kessler, David. A. *The End of Overeating*. Rodale Books: 2010.

Mollison, Bill with Reny Mia Slay. *Introduction to Permaculture*. Ten Speed: 1997. (But there are many good beginning permaculture books out there now. Some are a lot more accessible than some of the earlier books on the subject.)

Nestle, Marion. *What to Eat*. North Point Press: 2007.

Pendell, Dale. *Pharmako* trilogy. (The revised and updated editions.) North Atlantic Books: 2010.

Russell, Scott. "Starting Smart: Calculating Your Energy Appetite." *Home Power* #102. www.homepower.com/sites/default/files/uploads/webextras/loadcalc.pdf

Sarno, John. *Healing Back Pain: The Mind-Body Connection.* Any edition.

Scott, Timothy Lee. *Invasive Plant Medicine: The Ecological Benefits and Healing Abilities of Invasives.* Healing Arts Press: 2010.

Stamets, Paul. *6 Ways Mushrooms Can Save the World.* http://www.youtube.com/watch?v=XI5frPV58tY, 2010.

Thompkins, Peter. *The Secret Life of Plants.* Any edition.

Todd, Kim. *Chrysalis: Maria Sibylla Merian and the Secrets of Metamorphosis.* Mariner Books: 2007.

Valenzuela-Zapata, Ana G. and Gary Nabhan. *Tequila: A Natural and Cultural History.* University of Arizona Press: 2004.

Wansink, Brian. *Mindless Eating: Why We Eat More Than We Think.* Any edition.

Weston, Anthony. *How to Re-imagine the World: a pocket guide for practical Visionaries.* New Society Publishers: 2007.

About the Author

Kim Antieau is the author of many books, including her novels *Coyote Cowgirl, Church of the Old Mermaids,* and *Ruby's Imagine* and the works of nonfiction, *Under the Tucson Moon* and *The Salmon Mysteries*.

Kim is currently creating The Wayward Arts, a place and organization to inspire people to envision and plan sustainable, imaginative, beautiful ways of living, loving, working, and playing by using stories and art as visionary jumping off points. She is also creator of We Are Here: Geography of the Heart.

www.ingramcontent.com/pod-product-compliance
Lightning Source LLC
Chambersburg PA
CBHW030053100526
44591CB00008B/134